E 71   30

M 3

Fót út
Rákospalota
Csömör-patak
Hungaroring   Szilasliget
Széphegytelep
elszabadulás útja
Szilas-patak
Kerepes
Csömör
Kerepestarcsa
Újpalota
Pestújhely
Árpádföld
Szabadság út
Kistarcsa
ri út
Szabadföld út
Nagytarcsa
Csömöri út
Rákosszentmihály
Cinkota
Sashalom
Füredi út
Veres Péter út
Mátyásföld
Örs vezér tere
Fehér út
Pécel
Rákos-patak
Rákosliget
Jászberény út
Kőbánya
Jászberény út   Pesti út
Pécel út
Vasalya út
Maglódi út
Sibrik M. út
Rákoskeresztúr
Rákoscsaba
Kőbánya-Kispest
Ferihegy
repülőtérre vezető
Rákoshegy
Rákoskert
Maglód   31
Hunyadi út
Kispest
Ecser
rösi út
erzsébet
Pestszentlőring
Sallai Imre út
Méta út
Ferihegy - 1
International Airport
Ferihegy - 2
Halas-patak
Pestszentimre
Üllői út
Vecsés
Vörös Hadsereg útja
Szentlőrinci út
ksár
Péterimajor
Gyáli-patak
Gyál
E 60
4
E 75
Budapest
M 5
4 km / 2.5 miles
50

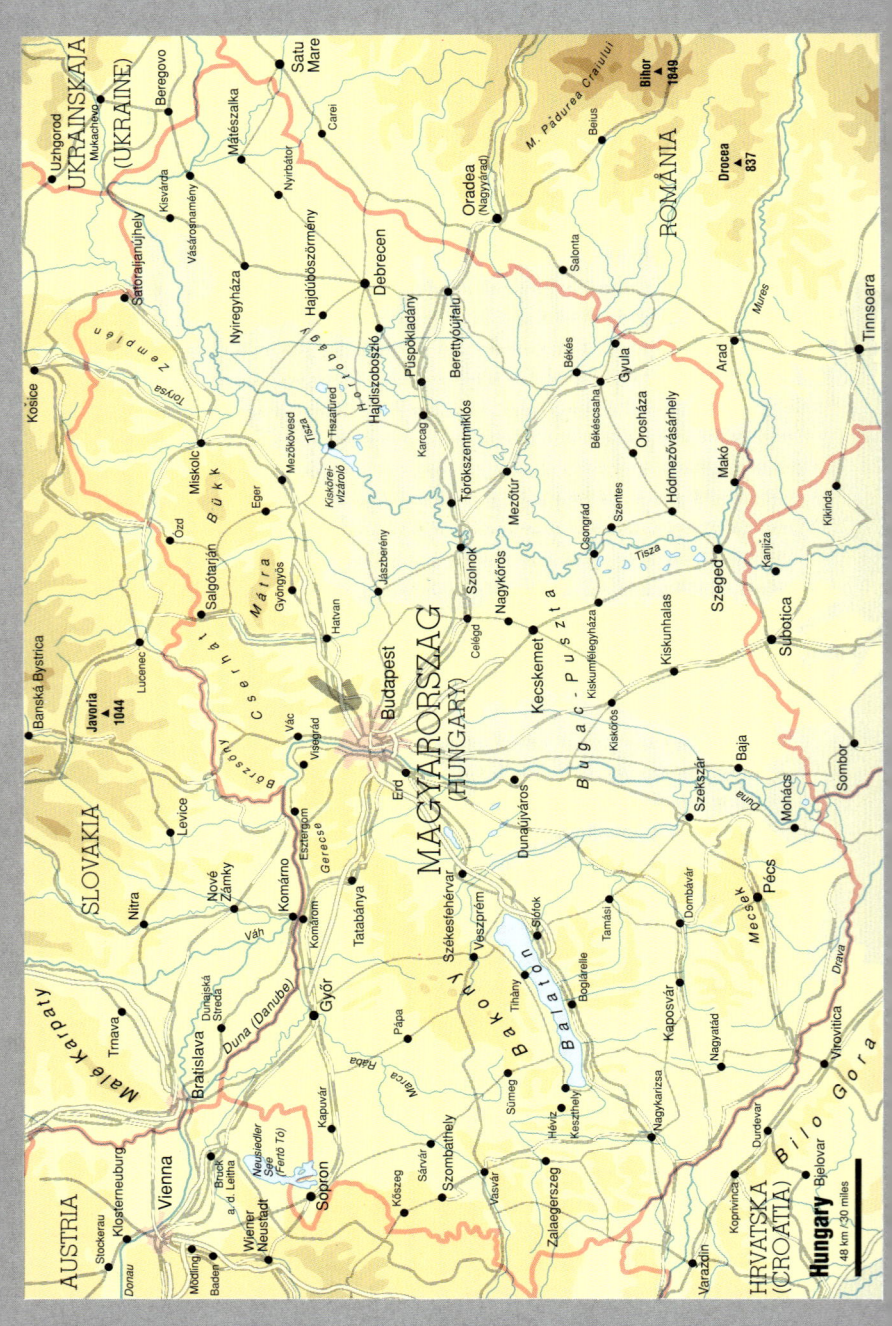

BUDAPEST
& SURROUNDINGS

Written and Presented by **Alfred Horn**

INSIGHT
POCKET
GUIDES

Insight Pocket Guide:

BUDAPEST

Directed by
Hans Höfer

Managing Editor
Andrew Eames

Photography by
Hansjörg Künzel

Design Concept by
V. Barl

Design by
Gaia Text, München

© **1993 APA Publications (HK) Ltd**

All Rights Reserved

Printed in Singapore by
Höfer Press (Pte) Ltd
Fax: 65-8616438

Distributed in the United States by
Houghton Mifflin Company
222 Berkeley Street
Boston, Massachusetts 02116-3764

Distributed in Canada by
Thomas Allen & Son
390 Steelcase Road East
Markham, Ontario L3R 1G2

Distributed in the UK & Ireland by
GeoCenter International UK Ltd
The Viables Center, Harrow Way
Basingstoke, Hampshire RG22 4BJ
ISBN: 9-62421-558-8

Worldwide distribution enquiries:
Höfer Communications Pte Ltd
38 Joo Koon Road
Singapore 2262
ISBN: 9-62421-558-8

Welcome! Once called the 'Queen of the Danube', Budapest, the capital of Hungary, has long been the focal point of the nation and a lively cultural centre. I have been visiting the city since the 1960s and have always been impressed by the atmosphere of comparative prosperity here, a marked contrast to the relatively drab appearance of most other Eastern European capitals I know. Even during the long decades of the Cold War, the city was the place to go for all those who wanted to take a peep behind the Iron Curtain without having to sacrifice too many of the amenities offered by city destinations in the West. Since the opening up of Eastern Europe in 1989 this particular attraction has largely been lost, and instead the tourists are now discovering the nostalgia of the Austro-Hungarian Empire in the city's coffee-houses and restaurants, its operetta and concert halls, and right along the Danube Promenade.

Together with my friend and advisor Zoltan Ivanij, who has frequently shown foreign visitors and friends around his native city, I hope not only to show you Budapest's more famous attractions, but also to introduce you to some hidden corners with their undiscovered restaurants offering high culinary standards. Budapest has often been described as a bridge between East and West; follow our trails through the city, in and out of its venerable coffee-houses and its magnificent thermal baths, and you'll soon begin to understand why.

We hope that after following these routes you'll have gained a good general impression of what the city is like: lively and colourful – in a word, Budapest!

Jó napot – Welcome! — Alfred Horn

Contents

Preceding pages:
Inside the Café Gerbeaud   **8**

Practical Information

Maps

9

Following pages:
the Parliament building

On 23 December 1992 Budapest celebrated its 120th birthday – the anniversary of the unification of Buda and Pest. But the metropolis on the Danube can actually look back on 2,000 years of history.

In the middle of the 1st century BC, the Celtic tribe of the Eravisci was already beginning to settle this area thanks to a ford over the Danube. They had been attracted by the 'Ample Water', and this gave the place its first name: *Ak-Ink*. The name became *Aquincum* a century later when the Romans built a military camp on the same site. Within the safety of the Roman walls a town sprang up that was elevated to the status of a *colonia* by Emperor Septimus Severus in AD198. But as the Roman Empire began to decline, so did the capital of the Roman province of *Pannonia* (West Hungary). According to the *Kriemhild Saga*, the only people who injected new life – albeit temporarily – into *Aquincum* around the year 450 were Attila the Hun and his brother Bleda. The Avars – a horse-riding nomadic people from the steppes of Asia – controlled the region for the next few centuries, and Slavonic tribes started arriving from the 6th century onwards.

In the 9th century the Magyars – also a nomadic tribe – appeared in the Pannonian plain. After a few vain attempts to progress further west, the Hungarians-to-be finally contented themselves with occupying the middle basin of the Danube. Their king, Stephen I (1000–1038) – later St Stephen – adopted the Christian faith, and his wife Gisela invited German immigrants to the country. New towns sprang up, and the rulers of the house of Arpád chose Esztergom, located on the 'knee' of the Danube, as their capital. The settlement of 'Pest' on the east bank, founded by Slavonic immigrants, gets its first mention in 1061. The name actually means 'lime kiln', and hints at the region's economic origins.

King Stephen I

Culture

In the year 1241 the Mongols – distant relatives of the Huns – overran the country and destroyed all the settlements that formerly stood on the city's present-day site. The terrified population fled to the safety of the limestone cliffs above the western bank of the Danube, and built a fortress there. However, the second attack they were expecting never actually took place, and the improvised refuge became a town in its own right. The Hungarians called it 'Buda', after the first constable of the fortress, the Germans knew it as 'Ofen'; what used to be *Aquincum* now became 'Óbuda' (Old Buda). It didn't end there, though: Pest, too, was rebuilt during the reign of King Béla IV, and the Golden Bull of 1244 even granted it full civic privileges. Development, however, concentrated on Buda. In 1276 King Ladislas IV granted it civic rights, and in the middle of the 14th century the Angevin kings set up court there.

Encouraged by the rulers, several new arrivals streamed into the town, among them many Jews, Serbs and Germans. The Hungarians were actually a minority in the town; only from the 15th century onwards did they make up more than half the membership of the City Council. This ethnic mix was not at all detrimental to Buda's industrial and cultural prosperity – quite the reverse, in fact. After the defeat of Prague as a result of the Hussite Wars, Buda developed into a full-blown European metropolis under King Sigismund, who went on to be elected king of Germany in 1410. The benevolent Renaissance humanism of King Mátyás Corvinus (1458–90) then allowed the city not only to flourish politically, but also turned it into a focal point of western learning and culture.

Turks and Christians

This period ended abruptly, however, with the triumphant onslaught of the Turks. After the Battle of Mohács (1526), the whole of today's Hungary fell under Turkish control for one and a half centuries. Hungary's nobles and bishops fled to today's Slovakia, and Poszony (today's Bratislava) became the capital of what was left of Hungary, while a Turkish pasha ruled in Buda.

Buda thus became a provincial capital within the Ottoman Empire, and it prospered. The Turks encouraged a sense of community and showed tolerance in their dealings with the population. A few

Christian churches, such as the parish church in Pest and the Church of Our Lady in Buda, were converted into mosques, but Christians and Jews were still allowed to practise their religions freely. The German settlers were expelled from the city, however – a preventive measure in the face of the Turks' continuing battles with the Habsburgs. The most visible and finest legacy of Ottoman rule in Budapest today are the city's magnificent Turkish baths.

The recapture of Budapest by the Christians was a far less pleasant affair. During the week-long siege in 1686 the city suffered heavy damage; when Duke Karl of Lorraine finally retook the fortress of Buda for the Habsburgs there were only around 300 people left, wandering through the ruins. Buda had to be founded all over again, and the other settlements in the area around the city continued to suffer for centuries. It was only in 1703 that Buda and Pest finally regained the status of free imperial cities.

The Habsburgs reigning in Vienna now donned the crown of St Stephen and ruled with an iron fist. It was not long, however, before the local population began to resist this foreign rule. From 1703 to 1711 the Hungarians, under Ferenc II Rákóczi, fought in vain against their erstwhile liberators. After his eventual defeat, Rákóczi was exiled to Turkey, where he died in 1735.

There was another uprising in Hungary in 1848, led this time by the radical Lajos Kossuth. The Habsburgs only managed to crush the revolution with the help of Russian troops, and they then went on to secure their hold on the recalcitrant city by building the Citadel up on the Gellért hegy. It now looked as if the reformist vision of Count István Széchenyi, a liberal, was doomed to failure: he had done his best to lead Hungary to autonomy by making a political compromise with the Austrians. His loyalty to the Habsburgs went unrewarded. They had him followed, and in 1860 went so far as to confront him with an alternative: to choose between being committed to an asylum or taking his own life. The Count chose the honourable way out.

His life's work outlasted him, however. The chain bridge, the construction of which he supervised, is merely the visible trace; the

Count also founded the Academy of Sciences, placing his entire annual income at its disposal; he speeded up the pace of industrialisation in the country; he had the Danube and the Tisza widened to accommodate more river traffic; he encouraged the construction of roads and railways; and he also had English thoroughbred horses imported – the ancestors of today's *puszta* horses.

In 1867 – seven years after Széchenyi's death – his political dream became reality. Under the Austrian foreign minister and later Reich Chancellor Count von Beust, the Austro-Hungarian Compromise came about, providing the basis

Chain Bridge, the Danube and Parliament

for the Austro-Hungarian monarchy. From now on, even though the crown of St Stephen was still being worn by a Habsburg, the Hungarians were in charge of their own country. This newly-won freedom was very soon exploited in order to 'magyarise' Slovakia, a region still happily referred to in Budapest even today as 'Upper Hungary'. Most of today's problems between Hungary and its small neighbour Slovakia have their roots in this historical development.

Independence

This political revaluation was like an elixir for Buda and Pest. In 1872 the twin cities were united, and Budapest was declared a royal capital in 1893. A 'Council for Public Works' brought order to the metropolis, which was already bursting at the seams. Traffic congestion was eased after the construction of the inner and outer ring-roads and also major radial streets such as the Andrássy út. The first ever underground railway in continental Europe, today's M1, was also constructed at this time. It led out to the monument that was unveiled in 1896 as part of the 1,000-year anniversary celebrations of the 'Magyar conquest of the country'. In 1903 the technologically impressive Elisabeth Bridge, Budapest's second, was built across the Danube. The architecture of these years of rapid industrial expansion is still a distinctive feature of today's city centre. The Opera House, the Parliament Building, hotels such as the Astoria and the Imperial, the Vigadó concert hall and the magnificent coffee-houses all bear witness to Budapest's economic prosperity at the turn of the century.

In 1918, however, as part of the Austro-Hungarian monarchy, Hungary found itself on the losing side of World War I. On 16 November a revolutionary body called the National Council assumed control of the republic. It collapsed, as did the soviet republic under Béla Kun that replaced it. On 16 November 1919, Admiral von Horthy, the last admiral in the imperial navy, used his 'national army' to seize power. But even this restoration of feudal structures in pseudo-democratic guise did not spare Hungary several painful territorial losses as a result of the war. At the Treaty of Trianon in 1920, the Allies deprived it of three-fifths of its land: Slovakia was incorporated into the newly-formed Czech and Slovak Republic, Transylvania was handed to Romania, and Croatia to Yugoslavia. Budapest, which had remained relatively intact during the war itself, was suddenly overrun by thousands of refugees from these territories.

Despite these problems, the capital of what remained of Hungary still continued to develop positively. Industrial production, encouraged by the opening of the International Free Harbour on the island of Csepel to the south, soon regained its pre-war level, and major public construction projects did much to alleviate homelessness and unemployment. In its attempt to break its foreign policy isolation, however, the Hungarian leadership ended up backing the wrong horse: the country became friendly with Fascist Italy and a

Communist march

short while later with Nazi Germany. Still hoping to win back the territories it had lost, Hungary finally took the side of the Germans in World War II.

When, on 15 October 1944, 'imperial administrator' Horthy attempted to free Hungary from German tutelage, it was too late: Hungary had already been occupied by the German army for months, and now the Nazi regime called on the openly Fascist Arrow Cross Party (Nyilas-Keresztes Párt) to form a puppet government. This resulted in a traumatic end to the war for Hungary, and especially for its Jewish population. Budapest was severely damaged in Allied air raids and artillery attacks, and in 1945 the retreating German troops blew up all the bridges across the Danube.

Communist Control

In November 1945, during the first free elections to be held for many decades, the 'Smallholders' party, with its social reform programme, received 57 percent of the vote. It also produced the country's first president, after the republic was declared on 1 February 1946. Meanwhile, though, the Communists were busy strengthening their influence behind the scenes. Having gained control of the police force, and with the support of the Red Army, they finally seized power in 1949. Stalin's henchman Mátyás Rákosi liquidated his critics within the party and led Hungary to Socialist tragedy.

In 1956 the people of Budapest rebelled. Demonstrators gathered beneath the statue of Hungary's greatest poet, Petőfi, to call for freedom of speech and socialist reform. They chose the Communist reformer Imre Nagy as their spokesman. Even the army, under General Pál Maléter, took the side of the demonstrators. This turned out to be too much, even for Kremlin reformer Krushchev. Soviet troops crushed the rebellion bloodily within a few days. Thousands died, and Nagy was executed after a show-trial in 1958.

Now it was János Kádár's task to administer the political and moral mess that remained. Proving himself a loyal vassal of the Soviet Union, he even sent two Hungarian divisions to Czechoslovakia in 1968 to end the 'Prague Spring'. As far as domestic policy was concerned, however, he was loosening the reins. His so-called 'goulash' Communism not only resulted in a marked economic improvement, it also created more freedom for science and the arts than in any other country of the lacklustre Eastern bloc. Thus it was no coincidence that the first proper 'hole' in the

A new identity

Iron Curtain appeared in Hungary – in 1989, when the new reformist Communist government allowed thousands of refugees from the former East Germany to escape to the West.

In 1990, while the West was still thanking the Hungarians for this courageous move, and Hungary's foreign minister Gyula Horn was presented with the European Charlemagne Prize *(Karlspreis)* in Aachen, the people of Hungary voted for a switch to radical conservatism in the elections on 25 March. Since then, a coalition government has plunged eagerly into privatisation of industry. But it isn't only in economic policy that the government, as well as its well-meaning critics, appears to lack a coherent strategy. The only noticeable shift has been back towards national and Catholic values. Doubts remain as to whether this will restore the domestic peace Hungary needs, and result in improved cooperation with its neighbouring states. The next elections are due to take place in 1994.

The Jews of Budapest

Jews have made an important contribution to the city's development ever since Buda and Pest were first founded. In the 13th century they played a major role in the stabilisation of the then newly-founded Hungarian Empire, and as a token of his gratitude King Béla IV granted them freedom of religion and full trading rights. Jews first began settling on castle hill before spreading to the rest of the city. As recently as the end of last century, around a quarter of the entire population of Budapest was Jewish. The unquestioning acceptance of Hungarians of Jewish faith into every area of public life only came to an end in the 1930s, when the Fascists seized power.

The Horthy regime had already been showing clear signs of anti-Semitism, but it was only towards the end of World War II that Nazi Germany, aided by the Hungarian *Pfeilkreuzler* party, began preparations for the liquidation of Budapest's Jewish population. It was only thanks to the courageous initiative of Raoul Wallenberg that the Nazis' plans for Budapest did not reach the same barbaric proportions they had elsewhere.

The son of a Swedish banker, Wallenberg had himself transferred to Budapest in 1944 as part of the

Raoul Wallenberg

Swedish legation. Once in Budapest he was confronted by Nazi butcher Adolf Eichmann, who was personally preparing the city's 'final solution'. After having persuaded the waverers in his own embassy to help him, he had the embassy issue a letter of safe-conduct announcing that 20,000 Jews in Budapest were henceforth to be treated as 'Swedish citizens'. He then set about purchasing several buildings to house the Jews, declaring them branches of the Swedish embassy. Wallenberg thus foiled the meticulously-planned deportations, and saved the lives of thousands.

During the final days of the war – Karl Adolf Eichmann had by this time moved further west – Wallenberg contacted the Supreme Commander of the advancing Red Army in order to organise a rehabilitation programme with him for Hungarian Jews. On 17 January 1945 he travelled to the headquarters of Marshal Malinovski, but was captured by the Soviets and deported. What happened to him after that remains a mystery to this day. The Soviet Union later issued an announcement that he had died in a camp in June 1947.

Life wasn't all that much better for the city's 120,000 Jews after the arrival of their 'liberators'. Even though they had only narrowly escaped the Holocaust, they were pushed around yet again and many were driven from the country. Today just 10,000 Jews still live in Hungary, most of them in Budapest's Erzsébetváros district, east of the Inner Ring Road.

The Turul

High up on Budapest's Freedom Bridge (Szabadság hid), a huge bird can be seen spreading its wings – it is the *Turul*, half-eagle and half-vulture, the totem of the Magyars. In their ancient lands – the steppes between the Volga River and the Urals – the bird brought them luck because it showed them the way to fresh pasture-land, and its scream warned them when enemies were approaching. For the traditional shaman, or *Táltos*, the bird was a source of wise advice. It thus accompanied the tribes on their wanderings as far as the Danube Basin, eventually to become the mystic symbol of history-conscious Hungary. On house facades and mountain peaks, sculpted from stone or cast in bronze, it stands guard over city and country.

Cultural Influences

Even though Hungary has been considered part of Western Europe ever since it adopted Christianity as its state religion around the year 1000, it has always been something of an outsider from the cultural point of view. One reason was certainly the Hungarian language, whose only (distant) relatives are Finnish and Estonian; it had to struggle for survival in the face of the Slavonic and Romance languages surrounding it.

Another reason was the relatively small number of Magyars in Hungary in the first place. Even during the reign of St Stephen at the beginning of the second millenium, foreigners – Ishmaelites, Jews, Serbs, and especially Germans – were being invited to settle the country. In the country's larger towns, actual Hungarians were quite often in the minority until as late as the 16th century. Then the Turks ran the country for 150 years, and when they were finally driven out, the Habsburgs of Austria treated Hungary as a colony for a further two centuries.

Little wonder, then, that an autonomous Hungarian culture only developed very late and with a great deal of difficulty. For a long time the very idea of a national culture was not entertained at all seriously by anyone outside the country, and even today Hungary's image abroad is still associated with gypsy romance, Lehár operettas and genuine Hungarian salami. This image in no way reflects the real state of things: Gypsies are not Magyars at all – in fact they probably came from Sind in present-day Pakistan. It was only around 1500 that reports began to arrive from Buda about 'lute-playing gypsies from Egypt'. Franz Lehár, born in

Traditional costume

1870 in the border town of Komárom, was mostly successful in Vienna, and he died in the Austrian town of Bad Ischl in 1948. Even the famed Hungarian salami actually first came from Verona, where the recipe then found its way to Hungarian butchers' shops. The country's spicy paprika, too, is a legacy of Turkish rule.

But never fear: despite the clichés, Hungarian culture is alive and well. The Hungarians have always been very open to outside influences, but visitors shouldn't hold that against them. Instead, you should admire the amazing skill with which they have managed to blend widely differing ethnic elements and cultural trends into an entirely new synthesis.

The poetry of the early Magyars – their ballads and shamanistic chants – was handed down by oral tradition and only survives today in myths and legends. A funeral oration dating from the beginning of the 13th century is the oldest surviving source of medieval Hungarian.

The earliest Hungarian writers, such as János Pannonius, the Bishop of Pécs (1434–72), used Latin as their language. It was thanks to Hussite (Czech) influence that the Bible was first translated into Hungarian at the beginning of the 15th century. In the centuries that followed, the written language was further refined by translators such as János Sylvester and Gáspár Károlyi as well as by the appearance in print of Hungarian grammars and Latin-Hungarian dictionaries. Bálint Balassi (1554–94) was the first poet to use popular Hungarian, developing his own style and verse form for his highly expressive songs of love and war.

Popular elements such as the *Verbunkos*, a traditional dance played when soldiers were being recruited, were central to the genesis of what can be referred to as 'typically Hungarian' music, which was further developed in the 18th century by violin virtuosi such as János Bihari and Anton Csermák. This is where Hungarian gypsy music, distinctive for its long introductions *(Lassú)* followed by its fast and syncopated dance sections *(Friss)*, has its roots. Franz Liszt (1811–86) considered this music to be 'originally Hungarian' and made arrangements of it in his *Hungarian Rhapsodies*. Liszt, who left his native Hungary as a child prodigy and achieved success in the Paris salons and as director of music in Weimar before

finally settling in Budapest and becoming president of the Academy of Music there, even wrote an article in 1859 entitled 'The Gypsies and Their Music in Hungary'.

His spiritual disciple Béla Bartók (1881–1945) was more painstaking altogether. Together with Zoltán Kodály, he collected more than 6,000 Magyar, Slovakian and Romanian folk melodies, and added their elemental rhythms to many of his greatest works. Bartók first taught as a professor at the Academy of Music in Budapest before emigrating to New

Franz Liszt

York in 1940, and his compositions, with their harsh dissonances and eruptive harmonies, made him a pioneer of modern music alongside Schönberg and Stravinsky.

Nineteenth-century Hungarian literature, too, went the same way, from Romantic to Modern. Ferenc Kölcsey (1790–1838), who wrote the national anthem, and Mihály Vörösmarty (1800–55), whose monument in Pest is inscribed with his *Ode to the Fatherland*, were models for the patriotic revolutionaries of 1848. Sándor Petöfi (1823–49), whose democratic verses found approval throughout Europe, became their martyr, and the popular folk hero *Toldi*, created by János Arany, became their literary myth.

Imre Madách (1823–64) was already sounding a different note in his poetic drama *The Tragedy of Man*: his protagonist, Adam the progenitor, is on the verge of despair when confronted with a speeded-up version of mankind's possible future. Only very reluctantly does he obey the divine command: 'Struggle and have faith!' While the brilliant novelist Mór Jókai (1823–1904) was enjoying success with his romances, Kálmán Mikszath (1847–1910) was developing into a master of ironic social criticism, later to be such an unmistakeable feature of the works of Zsigmond Móricz (1879–1942).

Petöfi statue

The literary periodical *Nyugat* ('The West') had a decisive influence on literary life in Hungary from 1908 to 1941. In her novel *Stations*, Margit Kaffka (1880–1918) described the first generation of the *Nyugat* circle and also elevated the emancipation of women to a literary theme.

The 1920s were just as 'wild' in Hungary as they were elsewhere, and are reflected in the work of Gyula Krúdy (1878–1933) as well as in the internationally famous operettas of Franz Lehár and Emmerich Kalmán. In contrast, Lázló Németh (1901–74) and Gyula Illyés (1902–83) depict the other side of the coin: social misery and rural drudgery. Through his work sceptical socialist Tibor Déry (1894–1977) denounces the absurder aspects of social development.

The Horthy era, World War II, Stalinist censorship and the gradual liberalisation under Kádár produced a handful of genuinely excellent cultural achievements. In literature, these include Erzsébet Galgóczi with her courageous novel *The Trap*, and the work of György Konrád, who was awarded the German Book Trade's Peace Prize in 1991 for his attempt to reconcile East and West.

The explosion of creative activity in painting, film and theatre – much of it acknowledged abroad, though rather belatedly in Hungary itself – is thus all the more remarkable.

Symptomatic of this development was the leading philosopher and social critic György (Georg) Lukács (1885–1971). Having graduated from the University of Budapest, in 1919 he became commissar for culture and education under Béla Kun's short-lived regime. He was then stripped of his title and forced to emigrate. In 1945 he returned to Hungary as an established Marxist cultural critic. An uncomfortable critic too, for he tended to regard artists not as soldiers of the party but instead as freedom-fighting partisans. Lajos Kassák, an all-round genius, and sculptor Imre Varga also never surrendered to the pressure that was exerted on them, and succeeded in retaining their artistic integrity.

Others only managed to give full vent to their talents once outside Hungary. These included abstract painter Victor Vásárhelyi, who achieved fame as the founder of the Op art movement, and film-maker István Szábo who was among a very promising group of young directors in Budapest during the 1960s but only made his real breakthrough with films he shot abroad, such as *Mephisto* and *Colonel Redl*. Szábo concentrates on his native city once again, though, in his most recent film *The Magic of Venus*, a lyrical and graceful send-up of the problems faced by a conductor who has to commute between Budapest and Paris.

Today the city offers an incredibly exciting art scene in which international influences combine with the talent of local artists to produce numerous original cultural highlights.

Sculpture by
Victor Vásárhelyi

Historical Highlights

1st century BC Celts found the fortified village of *Ak-Ink* at the hot springs on the western bank of the Danube.

AD198 The Roman provincial town of *Aquincum* is promoted to the status of a *colonia*; 60,000 civilians and around 10,000 soldiers live in the area of today's Óbuda.

c 450 Attila the Hun takes up residence close to the city surrendered by the Romans.

896 The nomadic Magyars occupy the country.

1000 King Stephen (later canonised as St Stephen) makes Christianity the state religion. After receiving papal recognition, the Kingdom of Hungary becomes part of Western Christendom.

1061 First written reference to Pest, the settlement on the east bank of the Danube.

1241 After the Mongol attack, the settlers take refuge up on the hill above the west bank. This settlement eventually develops into the royal city of Buda.

1458–90 Hungary and its capital, Buda, flourish under King Mátyás Corvinus.

1526–41 After the battle of Mohács, the Turks conquer what was effectively today's Hungary. Buda becomes a Turkish provincial capital for the next 150 years.

1686 A Christian army recaptures Buda, destroying it in the process. The Habsburgs of Austria don the crown of St Stephen.

1703–11 Hungarian rebellion against foreign rule, led by Ferenc II Rákóczi.

1848–9 Aided by Russian troops, the Habsburgs successfully crush the Hungarian freedom-fighters led by Lajos Kossuth.

1867 The Austro-Hungarian Compromise is reached under Austrian foreign minister Count von Beust.

1867–1918 Under the Austro-Hungarian Dual Monarchy, the Hungarians are left in charge of their own country. Budapest, which was united in 1872, becomes an international city.

1918–9 After the defeat of the imperial monarchy, Hungary becomes a republic, but takeover attempts by the revolutionaries as well as the socialists both fail.

1919 'Imperial administrator' Admiral von Horthy takes power after Hungary is on the losing side in World War I. Hungary is forced to cede three-fifths of its territory to neighbouring states.

1939–45 Allied with the Axis powers, Hungary also loses World War II. In 1944 German troops occupy the country; Budapest is severely damaged.

1946–8 Again a republic, Hungary is ruled for two years by civic reformers.

1949 The Communists assume power.

1956 On 23 October, students in Budapest protest against Stalinist terror; large sections of the population and even the army join them. Soviet tanks crush all hopes of freedom. Imre Nagy, the leader of the reformers, is executed in 1958.

1956–89 János Kádár runs the country under the motto 'Those who are not against us are with us'. His much-maligned 'goulash' Communism in fact lays the political foundations of the peaceful revolution of 1989.

1990 On 25 March, Hungary votes a conservative majority government into power. Professor Antall takes over as leader of a coalition government.

Budapest does not *lie* on the Danube; rather, the river flows *through* the city, dividing Buda from Pest. This gives the metropolis its special flair, and of course it also makes it very easy for you to get your bearings: to the west, on the 'Buda' side, stands the Castle Hill with the Mátyás Church; further to the south is the Gellért hegy with its famous thermal baths. Víziváros (Water City) and Óbuda lie to the north, as do the ruins of the ancient Roman city of *Aquincum*.

It was on the eastern, 'Pest' side that the modern city first developed. Danube Promenade and Váci utca are the main shopping streets in the city centre; a little further to the north is the Parliament Building, in the middle of the administration district.

The city of Pest is encircled by the Inner and Outer ring roads. Large axial streets form the spokes of this system, the most famous of which is the Andrássy út, a tree-shaded avenue leading out to the City Park, the zoo and the Széchenyi Baths.

The city's three Metro lines are very sensibly laid out, and they all intersect at Deák tér in the middle of Pest. Further public transport is provided by the bus and tram systems. At their respective termini there are connections to the surrounding area via the suburban railway system, HÉV.

In fact, the only really confusing thing about Budapest is its railway stations. True, a lot of trains from Austria and Germany do arrive at the West Station (Nyugáti pályaudvar), but both it and the East Station (Keleti pályaudvar) – where trains from the west also arrive – lie on the Pest side, ie in the eastern part of the city. The South Station, on the other hand, which is where trains to Lake Balaton depart, lies across to the west, beyond the Castle Hill.

The magnificent bridges over the Danube, connecting the many islands with the urban area, are also unmistakeable landmarks. Margaret Island in particular, which has been laid out as a municipal park, is an oasis of tranquillity.

On Castle Hill

Explore the romantic streets of the castle quarter of Buda; the Mátyás Church and the Fishermen's Bastion, with its superb view of the city; a great meal at the Pest-Buda.

Budapest's Castle Hill is only 60m (200ft) above the Danube, but it dominates the city and affords a fantastic view of both the river and the city of Pest on the opposite bank.

Begin the day's walk on the piece of projecting wall above the road leading up the eastern side of the hill, near the funicular *(Sikló)*. Here you can enjoy your first unobstructed view of the city, and the Fishermen's Bastion and the Mátyás Church are also visible. The building behind you was once a Carmelite monastery, but after the dissolution of the order part of it was turned into a **theatre**, and it was here in 1790 that the first Hungarian-language drama production took place. The building's wooden supports collapsed in 1924, and it was rebuilt in 1978. Today it features regular

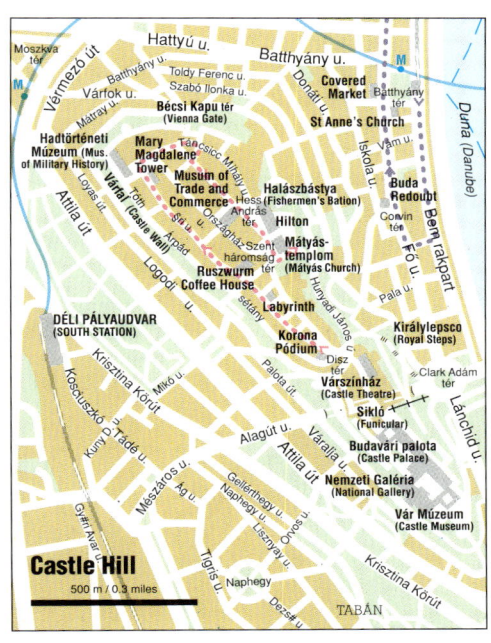

View of the castle

performances by members of the National Theatre. A good place for your first break is the **Corona Coffee House**, directly opposite. In fine weather the tables are also placed outside. Sit and contemplate the history of what surrounds you.

After the devastating Tartar raids of 1241, many settlers moved across from the unprotected side of the river to this long, rocky plateau in order to defend themselves better against the next attack. Even though that attack never actually came, the improvised refuge gradually grew into a town in its own right and became known as 'Buda', or 'Ofen' in German (most of the townspeople between the 13th and 16th centuries were German). The king's castle was built to the south, and the burghers built their houses to the north. After King Louis (Lajos) I (1342–82) chose Buda as his royal seat the city's rise to prominence as a European metropolis began – but it was then cut short by the Turkish victory of 1526 and by the occupation of the country by Pasha Suleiman II in 1541. The recapture of Buda 150 years later by the Christians reduced the city to ashes, and it had to be completely rebuilt thereafter. Buda's royal buildings, its churches and its houses thus nearly all date from the 18th century, even though most of them were built on earlier, medieval foundations.

A visit to the **castle building** takes at least two hours, even when its two museums (the National Museum and the Castle Museum) are just given fleeting glimpses, so I suggest you put that off until the afternoon, or until a second visit up here. The best way to get a real flavour of Budapest on your first day is to take an extended stroll through its castle quarter. The quarter contains four main streets running parallel to each other, connected by streets and passageways, and they all end at the square in front of the north gate. Even though it's impossible to get lost, proceeding relatively systematically is still a good idea.

From the Corona Coffee House, follow the **Promenade** that

In the castle quarter

leads up to the old fortifications surrounding the castle quarter. This avenue is lined by simple, rather inconspicuous-looking buildings; now and then you'll see the odd fine facade, attractive ornament or elegantly-executed archway, before arriving at a projecting bastion which provides the best view of the range of wooded hills to the south-west of the city, where the elite of the former regime and the *nouveaux-riches* of the capitalist era have their villas. The valley between contains the South Station and several noisy construction projects.

After the walk along the castle wall, take the parallel Uri utca. At No 9 you'll come to the entrance to the **Labyrinth**. As long ago as Turkish times, these limestone caverns under the hill were turned into a 10-km (6-mile) system of passageways and chambers, and they served as useful air-raid protection during the war. A handful of crafty young entrepreneurs now provide guided tours of the caverns and passageways, and have lined the route with papier-maché figures taken from Hungarian history, all of which makes the place a kind of cross between a geological-historical museum and a ghost train.

House No 19 on Uri utca, which once used to belong to the Italian campaigner Pipo of Ozora, contains a fine sundial in its courtyard and the only surviving street-bridge in the area. As soon as you reach the small square containing the equestrian statue of bold

The Promenade in autumn

hussar András Hadik – a former castle commandant of Buda and also a favourite of Empress Maria Theresa – you'll be greeted by your first view of the Mátyás Church across to the right. In the same direction lies the **Ruszwurm Coffee House**, famed even in Vienna, the home of great coffee-houses, for its delicious specialities.

But more of that later. Now it's time to admire the restored Gothic facade of house No 31. Then, at No 49, I recommend a peek inside the **Telephone Museum** with its array of exhibits documenting the early days of telecommunication. Finally you reach the rather isolated-looking **Mary Magdalene Tower**, which has now degenerated into a souvenir shop. Its former function becomes clear when one notices the wall foundations of the medieval **Franciscan Church** behind it. During the Turkish occupation this building served as a parish church for Hungarians living in the northern part of the castle quarter. Even the much reduced German congregation found room to worship here, and this resulted in a harmonious Christian solution: the Catholics were allowed to use the choir for their services while the Protestants were given the nave.

The broad square behind the Franciscan Church is flanked on the left by a former barracks, which today houses the **Museum of Military History**. To the right is the building housing the State Archives, and opposite is the Vienna Gate, which leads down to the Moszkva tér Metro station.

Mátyás Church reflected on the Hilton

At this point, however, turn right down Országház utca, or 'Parliament Street', named after the baroque building where the Hungarian Parliament used to hold its sessions in the early part of the 19th century. Today the building houses the **Hungarian Academy**, and the conference room here also doubles as a concert hall. The medieval houses at nos. 18, 20 and 22 will give you an idea of how the whole area must have looked centuries ago.

Turn left at the end of the Országház utca, and then left again off the small square of Hess Andrá tér to reach Fortuna utca, which runs parallel. At No 4 the **Museum of Trade and Commerce** contains several fascinating exhibits devoted to Hungarian cultural and social history over the past hundred years.

After visiting the museum, return to Hess András tér, named after the brilliant Renaissance printer. The monument here isn't of him, oddly enough, but of Pope Innocent XI. The building on the left of the square called the **Red Hedgehog** has been here since 1390. **Litea**, in a rear courtyard on the right-hand side of the square, has a fine selection of travel and art literature to browse through over coffee and cake.

Anyone after a more substantial meal will find it in the high-quality restaurant known as **Pest-Buda** at No 3, Fortuna utca (Tel: 1569 849, open daily), though in peak season you'll be lucky to even find a seat. An alternative is **Alabardos** at No 2, Országház utca (Tel: 1560 851) with its medieval atmosphere of Gothic arcades, lute music and candle-light. Less heavy on the senses, and cheaper too, is the **Fekete Hollo** at No 10, Országház utca (Tel: 1560 175).

Lunch-time!

You could also eat in one of the restaurants at the **Hilton Hotel** (Hess András tér, Tel: 175 1000). The Hilton was opened in 1976 and is definitely worth a visit anyway – seldom have medieval and modern styles been blended so harmoniously in one building. The objective during its construction was not to deprive any of the surrounding buildings of their effect: the cloister of the Dominican monastery was cleverly converted into a foyer, and is often brought to life by the concerts that take place there. The remains of a Gothic tower and what remains of the walls that once surrounded the choir of the church of St Niklas are the key elements that give the hotel facade its distinctive appearance. The various reflections of the surrounding buildings in the hotel's windows are also visually fascinating.

Next door, the **Mátyás Church** ironically enough has its modern neighbour to thank for the fact that it is so frequently visited. A century ago, its Early Gothic foundation walls received rather over-extravagant decoration. The most attractive aspect of the facade — rather one-sided in emphasis due to the high tower, which itself has no counterbalance architecturally — is its reflection in the mirror-glass of the hotel next door. Even the interior of the church exudes no sense of Gothic space. The wall-paintings are somewhat far-fetched, and light can only get in through the garish modern glass of the windows. The appeal of the church is external, a kind of backdrop, but it still nevertheless manages to enthrall locals and visitors alike. As old as Buda itself, it was being used as a parish church by the German population as long ago as the 13th century.

It received its present-day name in the 15th century because King Mátyás (Matthias) Corvinus was married here on two occasions. After undergoing a baroque conversion the church was restored in the Neo-Gothic style at the end of the last century. Architect Frigyes Schulek kept what few original fragments there were and invented the rest. This resulted in the 80-metre (260-ft) high tower, and the northern chapels with their colourful tile roofs. This kind of architectural mix can be seen elsewhere in Budapest too. You just take a pinch of everything: a spoonful of Gothic, a touch of Art Nouveau, a drop of neoclassicism and a lot of imagination; stir, add some colourful icing and serve, *et voilà!* The Budapest Romantic style.

The **Fishermen's Bastion**, next to the church, an amazing piece of kitsch, was also created according to this recipe. After Schulek had finished his work on the Mátyás Church he gave full rein to his architectural fantasies on the section of hill that had once been defended by the Fishermen's Guild. The finished end-product has even been copied by Disneyland. In 1906, when the construction work on the Bastion was finally completed, the mighty bronze **equestrian statue of St Stephen** was unveiled in the square. (By the way, the

The Mátyás Church, famous for its reflection

famous crown of St Stephen, Hungary's first ever Christian monarch, is on display in the National Museum; the one in the Mátyás Church Museum is a replica.) In the centre of the square in front of the church, at the highest point of the Castle Hill, stands the **Trinity Column**. This baroque masterpiece was created in 1713, during the plague.

The **Old Buda Town Hall** on the left at the corner, with its impressive entrance gate and its elegant flight of steps, also dates from that period. It was here that the heads of the city held their meetings from 1710 onwards, before moving on in 1873 to the combined town hall of the recently-united Buda and Pest. I would srongly recommend a visit to the **Pharmaceutical Museum**, a few steps further on beneath the square. Its three rooms house an alchemist's workshop containing all manner of mysterious paraphernalia and wondrous substances. The friendly museum attendants, all female, are keen to point out that no less a person than Hungary's reigning prime minister Antall wrote a learned brochure on the museum several years ago.

At this point you need to look at your watches. If you left out a visit to the castle building and its museums earlier this morning, you could embark upon one now (open until 6pm during the high season, but only until 4pm from 1 November onwards). Whatever you decide to do, I definitely recommend that you finish off the day by spending the evening at one of the restaurants mentioned earlier – dusk is the most romantic time of day in the castle quarter, when all the street-lamps come on.

If you want to take a different route back, take note: from the Hilton it's a ten-minute walk along the Táncsics Mihály utca to the Vienna Gate and down to Moszkva tér subway station. Just before you reach this lively square you will see a restaurant on your right-hand side that is famed for its excellent Russian cuisine: **Arany Kaviar** (Ostrom utca 19, Tel: 136 2917). On the corner directly opposite, the **Eden** discothèque, a popular meeting-place for young people in Budapest, opens its doors at 10pm.

The Fishermen's Bastion

Statue of poet Mihály Vörösmarty in Vörösmarty tér

DAY 2

Downtown in Pest

The centre of Pest; Vörösmarty tér, Váci utca and the Inner Ring Road, ending up with a delicious meal in the nostalgic atmosphere of the Astoria restaurant. A history tour or a shopping spree: the choice is yours.

– Metro station: Deák tér –

The city centre underwent a great deal of development work after the Austro-Hungarian Compromise of 1867, and soon it was bursting at the seams. However, despite all the extra construction, no further urban centres arose in the suburbs outside the Outer Ring. The heart of Pest thus remains the Belváros (Inner Town), and just as was the case a century ago, **Vörösmarty tér** is the main hub of activity; nearby Deák tér is where all three of the city's Metro lines intersect, and this is where this day's route starts.

Not all of the buildings on Vörösmarty tér are reminders of the glorious past, however: the very much purpose-built **House of Music** contains a concert hall, the largest music shop in the city, and an art gallery. The Art Nouveau buildings opposite are altogether more pleasing to the eye, and below them you can see the **Luxus** department store which until the economic liberalisation of the early

Take a break at Café Gerbeaud

1980s used to be the best in the city for quality and variety. Today it is privately run, and still considered a good address.

At the other end of Vörösmarty tér is the venerable **Café Gerbeaud**, the ultimate nostalgic Budapest coffee-house. Founded in 1870 and taken over by Swiss confectioner Emile Gerbeaud in 1884, the café is justly famous for its home-made specialities and the superb atmosphere of its three elegant rooms. There is also a terrace outside in the summer months.

The centre of the square is taken up by the monument to the poet **Mihály Vörösmarty** (1800–55). The Romantic patriot is surrounded here by several stone 'groupies' as he declaims his *Ode to the Fatherland*. The first verse is hewn into the plinth of the statue: *Love and loyalty to the fatherland in you, O Hungarian, ever shall remain!*

To stop the Carrara marble from cracking, the monument gets wrapped in plastic sheeting during the winter months. Then in springtime it gets unpacked once more, and the square is transformed into a summery market-place filled with portrait-painters, travelling traders and break-dancing children.

In contrast, there's always something happening the whole year through in the nearby pedestrian precinct, **Váci utca**: during the

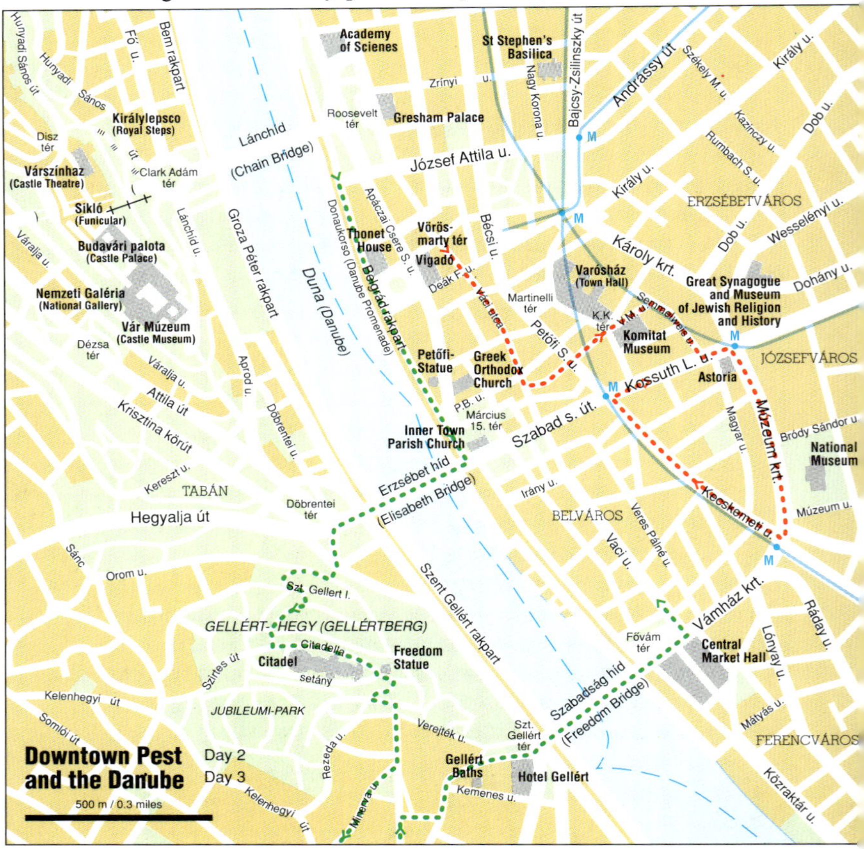

Downtown Pest and the Danube

500 m / 0.3 miles

Day 2
Day 3

Populous and popular – the Váci utca

daytime because of the kilometre-long row of exclusive shops there, and in the evening too, because this street and the smaller ones leading into it are not only lined with traditional hotels, restaurants and pubs but also contain bars, gambling dens and nightclubs. The boulevard is filled with the most colourful people at almost any time of day, among them the *Erdélyiek*, Hungarian emigrants from Romanian Transylvania trying to keep their heads above water by selling colourful hand-woven materials, embroidered cloths, furs and leather goods.

Strolling along Váci utca not only acquaints you with the bustle of the big city, it also gives you several glimpses into its history. At the first side-street you come to are signs of the former medieval town wall which marked the municipal border of Pest until 1789. It was then that the area around the tower known as the **Váci kapu** became so crammed that both it and the walls had to be pulled down. Today a white mark on the plaster recalls where the original city limits used to be.

Take time to examine house No 9 on Váci utca: this building still boasts a very striking Art Nouveau interior, which the flower-shop Philantia has made the most of. Pause at this stage for a short breather by the **Hermes Fountain**, with its elegant statue. Then it's off again until you see the International Trade Centre with its shopping arcade, opened in 1985, on the right. On the left, postmodern architecture made something of a late start in Budapest in the shape of the Hotel Taverna, built in 1985.

Souvenir?

Váci utca finally finishes up at the **International Bookstore**, and one block further on, on the level of No 28, is an antiques shop which also gets a mention in tomes dealing with the history of philosophy, for its well-stocked shelves were very popular with philosopher György Lukács, who spent the last years of his life in this area.

When you get to the ramp leading up to the **Elisabeth Bridge** *(Erzsébet híd)*, it's time for a good meal. A few steps away towards the Danube is the highly enticing

Even sewers reflect the splendour of the Budapest's past

Százéves, at No 2, Barnabás utca (Tel: 118 3608). The oldest restaurant in Pest, it is housed in a fine baroque building and since its anniversary in 1931 has been referred to respectfully as 'The Centenarian'. The atmosphere here in the spacious rooms with their open fireplaces is highly congenial, and there's a garden terrace in the summer. The game dishes and the wine here are both excellent.

After your meal, head back to the Váci utca, and on the other side of the street turn down the **Haris köz**. Roughly translated, *Köz* means 'narrow passageway', and this one certainly is, running between two buildings that look like watch-towers. Around the turn of the century a speculator opened up this little alley to the public to make his property increase in value. However, so as not to lose his ownership rights, he was forced to close off the passageway for at least one day each year. Running parallel to the Haris köz is the magnificent **Pariz shopping arcade**, which can be reached from all sides of the block including the Haris köz.

The Haris köz now becomes the Pilvax köz. It was here in March 1848, in the **Café Pilvax**, that the revolutionaries gathered and decided on their radical programme for national independence.

You will emerge into another square. The left-hand side of this, Kamermayer Károly tér, which contains the statue of the first ever mayor of united Budapest, is dominated by the massive **Town Hall**. The building began its existence as far back as 1711 as a home for invalids, and was later used as a barracks before finally being converted into the city's main administration building in 1894. The right-hand side of the square is dominated by the almost equally massive **Komitat House**, the administration centre for the country's 14 regions and five major cities. Virtually the whole of Hungary is run from here, for regional self-government is still practically non-existent in the country – even after the recent peaceful revolution. Almost everything of importance in Hungary still gets decided in Budapest. As well as its distinctive-looking facade on Városház utca, the Komitat House also possesses two magnificent inner courtyards where classical concerts are held during the summer months – usually on Monday evenings.

The end of the square is taken up by the elegant **Design Centre** building. Keeping to the right, you should now enter Vitkovics Mihály utca, where there are several charming shops selling hats, furs, gloves and jewellery. The **Galerie Bar**, with its discreet atmosphere, is a good place for a short break.

On Semmelweis utca, one of the few inner-city avenues to have been preserved, keep to the right, following it as far as the busy Kossuth Lajos utca. The impressive-looking house on the corner here was a Soviet cultural centre until very recently, and its present owners, still Russian, are now using it for commercial purposes.

The Kossuth Lajos utca and the **Inner Ring** (consisting of Károly körút and Múzeum körút) form the main traffic junction in the city centre.

Before taking the pedestrian subway beneath this junction, pay a visit to the **Gulácsy Art Gallery**, Károly körút 6. Founded in 1983, it was one of the city's first private galleries, and the 21 artists who run it see themselves as a diverse creative community with an aim rather than as a group of artists with the same outlook. The works on display are not devoted to any one single style or specific theme, and it is this very feature that allows the visitor such a comprehensive insight into the art scene of present-day Hungary.

The National Museum

Directly opposite stands a huge, glass-covered and architecturally very impressive building – one of the most up-to-date business centres in Budapest. It is a kind of department store *par excellence* where you can buy anything from a luxury car to a ready-made factory. The Hungarian government and Western investors are obviously very keen on turning Budapest into the hub of trade and investment within the former Eastern bloc. State-of-the-art office blocks like this are springing up like mushrooms all over the city.

The **Hotel Astoria** is on the other side of Kossuth Lajos utca. Even though its three stars have faded somewhat, its café and restaurant have retained their turn-of-the-century atmosphere. Everything is wonderfully old-fashioned, and of course a *Primas* performs with his gypsy orchestra here every evening. It's worth having at least one evening meal here just to experience that. In peak season it's a good idea to reserve your table (Tel: 117 3411, hot food noon–3pm and 6.30–11pm), and since you're here right now why don't you go and see the head waiter and do just that (an hour in advance usually suffices). A good alternative is the more traditional **Csendes** (on the Múzeum körút; enter via a side street, at Ferenczi István utca 3; open noon–10pm except Sunday; Tel: 117 3704).

You can now continue with your stroll until supper-time. Along

The Komitat House

the Múzeum körút keep to the right, and a few hundred yards further on you'll find yourself in front of the neoclassical portico of the **National Museum**, famous for its local history exhibitions. Note two very good antiques shops on the right: the **Központi Antikvárium** at No 15, and opposite the museum the **Honterus Antikvárium** at No 35. The Múzeum körút leads into Kálvin tér with its elegant **Reformed Church**. Pass under the so-called 'Bridge of Sighs' which connects two buildings belonging to the **Hotel Korona** on Kálvin tér, and turn right into Kecskeméti utca. This street, lined with impressive and well-preserved houses dating from the period of rapid industrial expansion at the end of the last century leads to the **University Church** – its baroque splendour unfortunately somewhat marred by the hotel buildings surrounding it.

Return to Kossuth Lajos utca by passing the Károlyi Palace and carrying straight on along Károlyi Mihály utca. On the corner stands Pest's inconspicuous **Franciscan Church**, built in Italian baroque style. The church door is adorned with the symbol of the Order showing St Francis of Assisi and the bleeding hands of Christ, and on the left-hand wall as you go in is a large plaque commemorating the devastating floods of 1838. If you now follow the busy Kossuth Lajos utca, keeping to the right, you'll get back to the Astoria for dinner. Another option would be to take the underpass back to where you started the day, on Váci utca.

Along the Danube

A stroll along the Danube Promenade and across the Elisabeth Bridge to Gellért hegy and the famous Gellért Baths, then back over Freedom Bridge into Váci utca, with its large choice of restaurants and shops.

The **Danube Promenade**, running between the Chain Bridge and the Elisabeth Bridge on the Pest side of the river, was once Bu-

The Danube Promenade can be positively Mediterranean when the sun shines

The Vigadó

dapest's biggest attraction. In the late 19th and early 20th centuries elegant hotels with such sonorous names as Carlton and Ritz lined the bank of the Danube here, as did many gourmet restaurants and coffee houses. Cosmopolitan society used to meet outside the cafés, and many people took their constitutionals along the banks of the Danube – not just the upper classes, but also locals from the suburbs, penniless Bohemians, adventurers and ladies of ill repute. All this apparent calm was shattered for ever in the hail of bombs during World War II, and after the destruction had ceased no-one had either the ambition or the imagination to rebuild what had been lost. The people of Budapest and their guests have thus had to content themselves ever since with a comparatively pale reflection of the Promenade's former glory.

If you've already visited the **Café Gerbeaud** on Vörösmarty tér you'll recognise the two Danube Promenade buildings dating from the good old days. The **Vigadó** was opened in 1865. The Hungarian word conjures up images of happiness and enjoyment, but despite its seductive name the Vigadó is nothing more than a rather majestic concert hall, decorated in an overly imaginative and colourful manner by architect Frigyes Feszl – a typical example of the mix of styles one so often encounters in Budapest. Music lovers waited patiently from the end of the war until 1980 for it to be reopened, but opinions were divided straight after the very first concert. The audience was enthralled by the magnificent setting that had been so painstakingly restored, but the musicians started to complain almost immediately – just as they had done 100 years beforehand – about the poor acoustics in the hall, which is nearly 20m (65ft) high. The people of Budapest adore the place nevertheless, and all its 640 seats are regularly sold out for each concert here. On New Year's Eve programmes featuring extracts from Hungarian operettas, entitled *Live From the Vigadó*, have been transmitted Europe-wide via satellite.

On the left-hand side of the rear stalls, a restaurant has been set up, but far more interesting is the famous modern art exhibition hall, situated in the right wing of the building. Nothing is actually for sale, but anyone lucky enough to have his work exhibited here can be sure of provoking a reaction country-wide.

The attractively laid-out park of the Vigadó is the central point of the Promenade. Further upriver, just one of what once used to be an unbroken row of neoclassical *palazzi* still

Refreshment

exists. The **Thonet House** contains several restaurants and comfortable cafés. Here, you can get an impression – albeit a modest one – of the luxury and glory of former days. After that, everything becomes functional again: the **Forum** and **Hyatt** hotels next door are both incredibly ugly concrete blocks, stuck above the Danube without any attempt having been made to integrate them into their surroundings, and with no sense of line or proportion whatsoever. Even the stylish interiors of both hotels cannot make up for these aberrations of 1980s architecture.

Further up the Danube, though, things get even worse: the **Hotel Duna-Intercontinental** is an accurate reflection of the soulless architecture of the 1960s – it is really nothing more than a suburban block of flats dolled up to look like a luxury hotel! I would advise giving its terrace a scornful miss, despite its fine view, and continuing with your stroll.

Next is a small park containing the statue of the poet **Petőfi**. Petőfi, a freedom-fighter, read out his poem *Talpra magyar* ('Rise, Hungarian') in the nearby café Pilvax, simultaneously sparking off the 1848 revolution and giving the Hungarians' struggle against the Austrians a poetic *leitmotif*. On 23 October 1956, when hundreds of students gathered next to this memorial statue and demonstrated against the Soviet Union and its puppet, Rákosi, Petőfi's patriotic poem was once more of burning relevance. During the ensuing procession past the Hungarian Radio building the first shots were fired on the peaceful demonstrators, resulting in the first fatalities of the revolution that was so bloodily crushed.

Beyond the park stands the **Greek Orthodox Church**, with its magnificent iconostasis. Its construction between 1791 and 1794 was financed by Greek merchants. Visitors are welcome to the services here, which are held in Hungarian even though they correspond to Greek ritual.

A banal-looking baroque facade, which is rendered even less impressive by the fact that it is situated right next to the six-lane ramp of the Elisabeth Bridge, actually hides the most interesting church in all Budapest. The **Inner Town Parish Church** (Belvárosi plébániatemplom) is worth seeking out. It began life back in the 13th century as a three-aisled Romanesque cathedral, and was then extended during the Gothic period. Its long choir, complex ribbed vault and also some of its windows have been preserved despite wartime bombs. The Turks used this church as their Friday mosque, and the niche where they prayed, the *Mihrab*, can still be seen.

In front of the church, excavations have revealed the foundations of a **Roman military camp**. Advance guard-posts of the Roman province of Pannonia protected this strategically very important spot in the city where the Danube reaches its narrowest and most crossable point (285m/930ft).

Now cross over to the Buda side of the river. Today's **Elisabeth Bridge** (Erzsébet híd) is a modern construction that was only opened to traffic as recently as 1964, because the retreating German troops blew up this bridge – along with the others – in 1945. All that could be safely salvaged from the previous bridge, which had been completed around the turn of the century, were its piers. These are traversed by the thick strands of cable which individually support the 27 different sections of the structure.

The **Gellért hegy**, a massive, tree-covered limestone cliff which will now be towering above you, was named after Bishop Gellért (Gerhard) of Csanád, a missionary who was tied to a cart and pushed off the edge of the steep cliff here by several furious Hungarians, who had no interest in complying with their king's request to join the Christian faith.

The descent is rather more gentle today, however; it takes around 20 minutes to complete and winds its way down via several stone stairways and paths. At the first terrace you'll see the **Saint's Monument**, framed by its colonnade – histrionic and altogether rather nasty, just like most other turn-of-the-century monuments. Then continue on to the **Citadel**, which was erected by the Austrians as a military bastion to keep an eye on the city and the hill after the Hungarian freedom-fighters were defeated in 1848–9. There is a restaurant and café up here – this once forbidding fortress has now become a major tourist destination.

The **Freedom Statue** on the viewing terrace, erected in 1947 – in the shape of a woman holding an olive branch, and visible for miles around – is a reminder of the end of the tyranny of national socialism. From there descend through a former vineyard to the

Hotel Gellért, taking a minor detour in the park on the way down to admire a few of the fine villas along the Minerva utca – and especially the studio house at Kelenhegyi út 12–14. This brings you down to the open-air swimming-pool, generously extended over the years in the same architectural style, which with its wave-bath provides a summer addition to the renowned indoor thermal Turkish baths themselves; these are open all year round (6.30am–8pm; closed Sunday afternoons). The Turkish baths and the massage rooms have separate

Bathing at the Hotel Gellért

sections for men and women. The entrance fee is 200Ft; access to the Turkish baths costs a further 200Ft; a 10-minute massage costs 120Ft. Don't forget to pay for everything on your way in, otherwise you'll be sent packing.

In contrast to its dazzling Art Nouveau swimming bath inside its spacious, glass-roofed hall, the 'luxury hotel' part of the Hotel Gellért has looked rather grim and disappointing ever since its restoration during the 1960s. The restaurant, too, isn't as cosy as it could be, although the food is absolutely superb (Tel: 185 2200).

Cross back over to the Pest side of the river via the **Freedom Bridge** (Szabadság híd), which was built in 1896. It is certainly the finest of the three bridges in the city centre area, and reflects all the exuberance and sheer variety that characterises turn-of-the-century Hungarian architecture.

On the other side of the bridge, the promenade is dominated by the neo-Renaissance building housing the University of Industrial Science – formerly the customs house for the river harbour. Right behind it is the **Central Market Hall**. This began to flourish as a modern market around the turn of the century, and deliveries to it could even be made direct from the Danube, via an underground canal. Here, in a shopping area covering a length of 150m (500ft) along galleries and various side annexes, the buyer can find every conceivable type of Hungarian produce, and of course imported exotic fruit too. Some very thorough renovation work began here in the winter of 1991, but even then none of my friends in Budapest believed that the projected date for re-opening – 1 June 1992 – would ever be kept. Sure enough: they were still busy with the extension work during the spring of 1993.

Opposite the Market Hall is the upper section of **Váci utca** – the southern 'poor relation' of the far more affluent northern part of the street. For a long time this part of Váci utca was neglected by the Budapest town planning department, but after it was finally closed to through traffic in July 1992 it very soon became an elegant shopping street. This does it more than justice historically, too, because this quarter is part of what once used to be the very heart of Pest, as evidenced by the still-surviving remains of the medieval town wall in the parallel street, Veres Pálné utca. Thus, a relaxed stroll down this street is definitely to be recommended. There are still a few junk shops and some genuine Hungarian pubs hidden behind these fine houses with their run-down facades, but new shops and restaurants keep springing up between them too.

One shop that is definitely worth a visit is **Antiquities** which is located in the basement of house No 66, with its fine selection of old furniture, carpets and lamps. The lady who owns it will patiently and charmingly explain to you why the best exhibits aren't quite as cheap as they were just a few years ago — real bargains are just as hard to come by in Budapest nowadays as they are anywhere else.

The stylish **Hotel Nautilus** at Váci utca 72 (Tel: 1384 830, open noon–2pm) is my tip for a fine supper this evening. The menu in English and German features all manner of seafood in very imaginative variations, but there are delicious meat dishes too: try *Breast of Turkey in Roquefort Sauce*. Anyone in search of more substantial Hungarian fare should continue on to the **Restaurant Nautilus** which is in the large block at the end of the same street; there's a casino next door where you can try your luck afterwards and — who knows? — maybe even win back the price of the excellent meal you've just enjoyed.

The Freedom Bridge

Option 1. József nádor Square

Highlights of 19th-century urban architecture in Pest; walk out onto the Chain Bridge.

– Metro: Deák tér –

This itinerary begins at **József nádor tér**, the square right behind the Café Gerbeaud on Vörösmarty tér. In the centre of this noisy, traffic-filled square lies a small park containing the mighty statue of the archduke Joseph, who ruled Hungary for half a century. Also on József nádor tér note the **Gross House**, built in the neoclassical style in 1824. Next door, a shop specialising in world-famous Herend Porcelain has recently opened its doors. The **Derra House** on the north side of the square, originally built for a rich Greek merchant, is also of architectural interest. Now turn left down J. Attila utca, the street that runs past the finely-restored facade of the Derra House, to arrive at Roosevelt tér, a square laid out as a park, which leads on to the Chain Bridge.

On your right here stands the finest Art Nouveau building in the whole of Budapest with the very un-Hungarian name: the **Gresham Palace**. The London banking and insurance company of the same name moved into this building, designed by Zsigmond Quitter, in 1906. The owner had himself immortalised in a larger-than-life bust. On sunny afternoons the facade lights up and the whole building is surrounded by a kind of golden aura. Unfortunately, the magnificent iron gates and the domed hall are the only real re-

Sikló funicular

minders of its former splendour. During the decades of Communist rule the building fell into disrepair, and when even the new city council was unable to raise enough money for its restoration it was sold to foreign investors. Since the deal included no promises to improve the look of the place, one can only hope that the new owners of this jewel will do it justice by restoring it to its former splendour.

The **Academy of Sciences** on the northern side of the square, founded in the middle of the last century, has had

The Chain Bridge

an altogether happier history, as is clear from its well-preserved exterior. However, the internationally-acclaimed President of the Academy, who secured its independence from party politics in 1990, decided to throw in the towel because of the disappointing economic situation in Hungary and accepted the offer of a chair at Harvard.

The **Chain Bridge** (Széchenyi lánchíd) has connected the twin cities of Buda and Pest since 1860. If you walk across it to the other side of the Danube you can either take the Sikló funicular up to the castle and visit the sights you skipped on *Day One* (the castle and its museums) or take a stroll along the highly panoramic promenade beside the river. Turning left will bring you to the Hotel Gellért, and to the right lies the district of Víziváros or Water City, which is explored in more detail in the next optional itinerary, *The Danube and Király.*

The Chain Bridge

The **Széchenyi Chain Bridge** (Széchenyi lánchíd) was the first proper bridge to link the two halves of the city and a metaphor for unity at the time it was built. Today it forms the main traffic artery between the city and Castle Hill. It is particularly impressive at night, when its spans and pylons are illuminated.

This bridge – the symbol of the city – is a true masterpiece. The Danube is nearly 300 metres (1,000ft) wide at this point, and 200 years ago a skilful method of spanning it needed to be found. The townspeople had been using a pontoon bridge ever since medieval times; occasionally, during icy winters, it was possible to walk across to the other bank. The problems started whenever the level of the Danube rose; the pontoon bridge had to be pulled in very quickly, and not even ferries could cross over because of the powerful current. One account of the winter of 1800 relates how the municipal authorities of Pest were stuck in Buda for weeks on end, because of flooding. They had come over for the palatine's wedding celebrations when a sudden thaw cut off their return.

A few years later Count István Széchenyi devised a remedy: he formed a society to promote the construction of a bridge, and two English engineers, Adam and William Tierny Clark, created the suspension bridge. To foot the bill, the state parliament decided to impose a general toll on anyone using the bridge – much to the anger of the nobility, who were effectively being asked to pay tax for the first time in their lives. Construction work on the internationally-acclaimed bridge, with its span of 202m (660ft) from pier to pier – an incredible distance for that time – could thus be successfully completed between 1839 and 1849.

Mosque-Tomb of Gül Baba

Option 2. The Danube and Király

Along the Danube Promenade on the Buda side at the foot of Castle Hill, with visits to the Király Turkish Baths and the Mosque-Tomb of Gül Baba, all in the Víziváros district.

– Metro M2: get off at Batthyány tér –

Walk upstream from the Buda side of the Chain Bridge, until you come to **Batthyány tér** (it can also be reached directly on the M2 metro line), a square which is dominated by the twin towers of the **Church of St Anne**. Up on the facade of the church, the sculptured figures of St Anne and The Virgin as a child can be seen. The interior is restrained baroque, with a magnificent altar in the middle and a fine-sounding organ up in the loft – although you'll have to time your visit carefully to actually hear it.

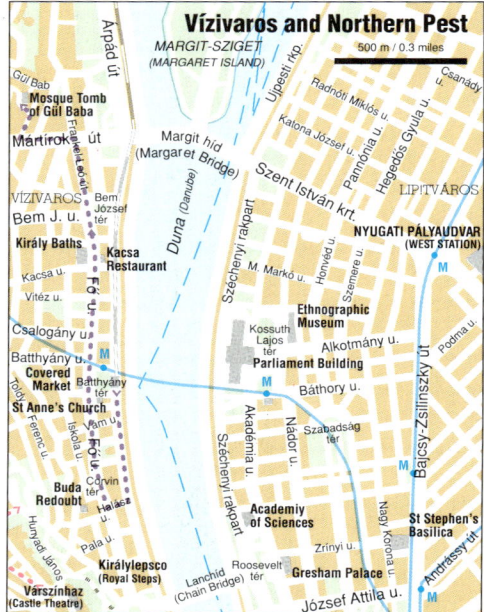

To the right of the church is a **market hall** that is definitely worth a visit: even before economic liberalisation was first introduced rather hesitantly two decades ago, this place was doing great business. Today it is an ABC supermarket, but still has a huge range of goods available.

In the direction of the Danube, the spacious but still very cosy **Café Angelika** can be found

The Király Baths

Not many traces remain of the 145 years of Turkish rule in Budapest, but the magnificent Király Baths are a wonderful exception to the rule. To reach the entrance on Fő utca you have to go down some steps, because today's street-level is a good 2 metres (6ft) higher.

At the ticket window you also need to pay in advance for your massage – there is a choice of either water or powder. I recommend the wetter version, where an enthusiastic masseur goes to work on you with warm water and curd soap. For the equivalent of about $3 you get given a changing cubicle on the first floor and also a small loin-cloth – the only article of clothing allowed when using the baths. (Fő utca 82–86. Men: Monday, Wednesday, Friday 7am–6pm; Women: Tuesday, Thursday 7am–6pm and Saturday 7am–2pm; closed Sunday.)

After the obligatory shower, the fun begins with the sauna. Things only really get going in the big steam-bath, though; you literally have to grope your way into this room with its domed ceiling because of the thick clouds of steam inside. Just beyond the entrance is the cold pool, and to the left of it the steam sauna, where the smell of sulphur has been rendered more pleasant by an agreeable camomile aroma. After your first bath you can relax in the chest-deep water of the warm pool, which is just large enough for a couple of swimming strokes, though most of the guests tend to slouch around at the sides. Whether or not you're a foreigner, this is the right place to strike up a conversation with the people of Budapest, with whom the baths here are a real favourite. By the way, the odd homosexual visitor may make gentle advances, which you can either reject or accept depending on your preferences. The same kind of thing apparently also takes place among the women who come here on ladies' days.

After the first session it's time for your massage, which it's best to have applied for in advance before entering the sauna so as to avoid having to queue up outside the room next to the showers. Dry towels are provided, as are deck-chairs and blankets in a quiet relaxation room on the first floor. A dry massage with powder is also available; anyone who feels like it can also have a manicure. After your second or third session in the baths, a fitness studio on the ground floor is available for muscle training (at an extra charge). All in all, a visit to the Király Baths will teach you far more about Budapest than any number of long walks.

The Király Baths, a welcome reminder of Turkish rule

on the ground floor of the presbytery. Poetry readings and other minor cultural events also take place here from time to time. In former times the café was an exceptionally popular rendezvous point for lovers and also supposedly for spies – several espionage scandals are said to have resulted from this potentially very explosive mixture. Spies of course are pretty thin on the ground in Budapest these days, but for young lovers who have just completed a stroll along the Danube Promenade, the Café Angelika is still a very popular destination.

Continue to follow the avenue of chestnut-trees along the Danube until you come to the Neo-Gothic **Reformed Church** with its slim brick tower. Because of its fine acoustics, the church's simple interior is often used for concerts and choral music, so it's worth taking a quick look at the notice-boards outside the entrance to see what's on.

In the next block there's an open-air cinema that shows films from 9pm onwards in the summertime. After passing the cinema, turn right into Halász utca (note the inexpensive restaurant called **Dunapart** on the corner, which is a good place to eat later on) before crossing Fő utca, which broadens out here into a small square lined by pretty baroque houses. The northern side of the square is dominated by the Buda **Redoubt** – Buda's answer to Pest's Vigadó concert-hall. There is a fine view from here of Castle Hill above, with the Fishermen's Bastion and the Mátyás Church.

Going along Fő utca, north of Batthyány tér, you will come to the **Király Turkish Baths** (Nos 82–86, Fő utca). There magnificent baths are divided up into 'men only' and 'women only' sections (see previous page for details of bathing times).

For those who aren't at all keen on the idea of a Turkish bath right now, this route continues walking northwards along Frankel Leó út; after passing the ramp leading up to the Margaret Bridge (Margit híd) which returns across the Danube via Margaret Island, turn left off this street along the narrow Gül Baba utca, lined with stylish houses and leading up to the magnificent **Rose Hill** (Roszádomb), with the **mosque-tomb** of the 'Father of the Rose', **Gül Baba**. Legend has it that this holy individual – who died in 1541 in the presence of the Turkish Sultan in the Mátyás Church – introduced rose cultivation to Buda. He was laid to rest in the middle of his rose-garden, and many Moslem pilgrims still make the journey up here to the attractively-sited tomb to pay their respects.

After your walk to Gül Baba's tomb or your Turkish bath at Király, a good place to meet up is the fine restaurant known as **Kacsa** (Fő utca 75, Tel: 135 3357), where international food gets served until late into the night, including the house speciality, roast duck. And then, dining over, it's a pleasant night-time walk back into town.

Option 3. Óbuda and Art

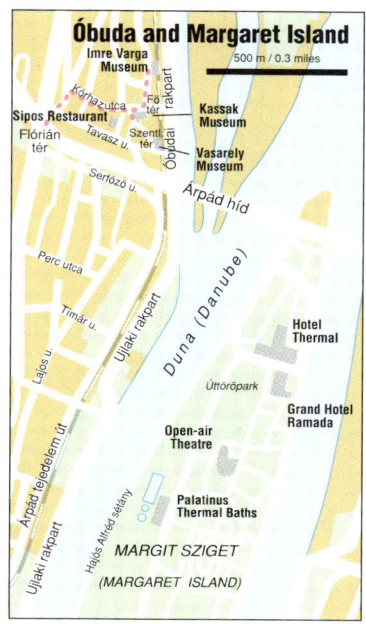

Óbuda and Margaret Island

Imre Varga Museum
500 m / 0.3 miles
Sipos Restaurant
Kórház utca
Fő tér
Óbudai rakpart
Kassák Museum
Flórián tér
Tavasz u.
Szentl. tér
Vasarely Museum
Serfőző u.
Árpád híd
Perc utca
Duna (Danube)
Tímár u.
Újlaki rakpart
Hotel Thermal
Lajos u.
Úttörőpark
Grand Hotel Ramada
Árpád fejedelem út
Open-air Theatre
Újlaki rakpart
Hajós Alfréd sétány
Palatinus Thermal Baths
MARGIT SZIGET
(MARGARET ISLAND)

Budapest's unjustly neglected 'third' city, with its old centre, and three fascinating museums.

– HÉV from Batthyány tér (via the M2) in the direction of Szentendre; get off at Arpád híd (Arpad Bridge) –

The third city next to Buda and Pest is Óbuda, the oldest settlement in today's metropolitan area and often the least visited – unjustly so, because Óbuda has quite a lot to offer.

True, when you get off the Metro at Arpád híd station you immediately feel like heading straight back again in the other direction when faced with the ugly blocks of flats and busy streets here. Stay calm, though: after walking a few steps off to the right in the direction of the Danube you'll reach the old market square, Fő tér – an oasis of tranquillity.

'Women with Umbrellas' by Imre Varga

Óbuda is *the* place to go for modern art in Budapest; most visitors, though, and even quite a few locals, have no idea what treasures have been compressed into this small area. The work of a great modern artist can be admired in the 18th-century palazzo at **Szentélek tér 1**, right next to the HÉV stop. The **Vásárhelyi Museum** contains an extensive collection of the work of abstract painter Viktor Vásárhelyi, born in Hungary and a resident of France since 1930, who achieved fame as the founder of the Op Art movement.

A second place for surprises is the **Lajos Kassák Museum**, tucked away in an inner courtyard to the right of the Town Hall Square. Kassák was an anarchist and a genius: a poet, publisher, painter and political agitator all rolled into one. Having trained as a metalworker, in 1909 he set out to discover the world and brought back new political ideas as well as strong artistic ones from Paris, Vienna, Frankfurt and Brussels. Cubism and Futurism influenced his formal language and also his cultural-political activity. He became a writer; he published left-wing magazines and also designed several highly controversial posters. His free spirit could not cope with the strains of socialist realism, however, and he thus gained far more acclaim

47

abroad, in the West, than in his native land. It was only in 1965, two years before his death, that he received the Kossuth National Prize, and his trailblazing literary work was finally given official recognition in Hungary.

The main square, **Fő tér**, is distinctive for its old town hall and an unbroken row of attractive town-houses. To the right there is another, smaller square containing a fascinating group of figures by Imre Varga entitled *Women with Umbrellas*. They point the way towards the **Imre Varga Museum**, at Laktanya utca 7, where I have always been particularly fascinated by his row of highly-decorated soldiers: the men stand there in their full finery, with their proud, medal-covered chests puffed out – but each one has a wooden stump instead of a left leg, a bitter attack on militarism, and extremely daring for an artist working under what at that time was still Communist rule. There are also some impressive pieces of sculpture in the garden, and over coffee the knowledgeable women who run the museum will be happy to provide you with more detailed information on the life and work of this internationally acclaimed artist, who represented Hungary at the Venice Biennale in 1984. Varga himself sometimes puts in a personal appearance at the museum – usually on Saturday around lunchtime – and chats with visitors for an hour or two.

Take a stroll through the various antique souvenir shops around Fő tér, where it's still possible to find quite a few unusual books, crockery and household articles which are unavailable anywhere else in the city.

As far as eating is concerned there is a choice of restaurants in Óbuda, and a particularly good one is the traditional **Sipos** (Fő tér 6, Tel: 188 8745), where extra tables are placed outside in the summer, inside a small courtyard. The chef's speciality is seafood – the harbour and the former fish market are just a few paces away. These days, however, this area is a lot quieter than it used to be. The shipyard installations closed down a long time ago, and the harbour basin today only contains the odd rusty barge.

From mid-April to the end of October this trip would be well combined with a detour to the old Roman city of *Aquincum*. All you need to do is take the HÉV a short distance further and get off at its 'Aquincum' stop.

Lada or Skoda?

The tomb of Lajos Kossuth

Option 4. Kerepesi Cemetery

A concentration of history and atmosphere in peaceful surroundings.

− Metro stop: Keleti pu −

A visit to the Kerepesi Cemetery is not only for those of a romantic or melancholy disposition, but also for those with a taste for history; here you will encounter every level of the city's past.

The cemetery, with its high trees and its nine hectares (22 acres) or more of land, contains Hungarians from every social class and of every cultural and political persuasion. Many of the graves are artistically interesting and some extremely bizarre; among them stands the tomb of honour of Lajos Kossuth, the revolutionary of 1848, who until 1894 actually lay buried in Turin. Even today, the tomb is still watched over by a guard who is happy to relate details from the great man's life to interested visitors.

Franz von Deák, who together with Count Ferdinand E von Beust engineered the Austro-Hungarian Compromise of 1867, also lies buried here.

Wander past the gravestones and decipher some of the inscriptions, let the atmosphere of the place sink in, and track down the odd famous name you may already have encountered on signs around the city: the confectioner Gerbeaud, for instance, founder of that fine café on Vörösmarty tér, or politician Lajos Batthyány (there's a metro station which you've probably already encountered with his name).

Those who don't feel that it's too irreverent should join many other Budapest natives and, equipped with picnic hamper and reading matter, spend a nice sunny day in the cemetery, interspersed with a few brief strolls around the monuments. By the way, the place provides terrific opportunities for photographers.

The city centre is just a short Metro trip away from the nearby East Station.

History lives on

From Vörösmarty tér through the northern part of the new town, then via József nádor tér and Nádor út to Kossuth Lajos tér, in front of the Parliament Building.

– Metro line 2: get off at Kossuth Lajos tér –

After emerging from the Metro, proceed northwards to arrive in the broad square known as **Kossuth Lajos tér**, named after the leader of the 1848 Hungarian Revolution; the statue of Kossuth can be seen in the northern part of the square. To the south is a monument to Prince Ferenc II Rákóczi, another Hungarian hero in the struggle against Habsburg rule. To the west stands a further symbol of national and democratic resistance: the **Parliament Building**, constructed between 1885 and 1902. Designed in Neo-Gothic style and influenced by the Houses of Parliament in London, this enormous edifice stretches a length of 268m (880ft) along the banks of the Danube, its 96-metre (314-ft) high dome towering above it. The white limestone facade radiates grandeur and nobility, and it is justifiably one of the most popular buildings in the city with photographers.

It can also be visited on request (information and applications for guided tours Tel: 112 0600). Those satisfied with just the exterior can head on to the **Ethnographic Museum** on the other side of the square. The building housing it was constructed at the same time as the Parliament building, and was formerly the headquarters of the royal law offices and the supreme court of justice. The frescoed ceiling of the monumental central hall still shows the figure of Justice with her virtuous and not-so-virtuous sisters.

The alternating exhibitions of cultural history and the permanent exhibition of Magyar folk art are both highly informative. The tour

The Parliament Building with its 96-metre dome

through the exhibition rooms, which are laid out on a thematic basis, begins on the first floor, over on the left. The highly intelligent women museum-keepers here mostly speak English, German or both, and do their best to answer all their visitors' questions.

For a quick snack, a good place to go is the **Delicatessen** on the south side of the square. Here, you can buy weighed portions of paprika sausage or spicy goat's cheese; the coffee is also excellent. You need to pay in advance and then hand in your receipt at the counter to receive your order.

Option 6. Margaret Island

A half-day walking tour with several gentle side-trips across this tranquil island in the Danube, plus a visit to the Palatinus Open-Air Thermal Swimming Baths and then, to finish off, a little snack at the Grand Hotel Ramada.

On Margaret Island

– No 26 bus from Nygati pu. If arriving by car, cross the Arpád híd (bridge) –

Situated between the two main bridges – the Margit híd to the south and the Arpád híd to the north – this fertile island in the Danube offers 2½ km (1½ miles) of shady parks, excellent swimming pools, romantic ruins, attractive cafés and elegant hotel-restaurants; just the place, in other words, for a hot summer's day. And even though it lies so close to both parts of the busy city centre, the island is an oasis of tranquillity during the other seasons of the year as well.

Margaret Island was used as a park, thermal bath and Danube fortress as long ago as Roman times. In those days it was connected to the Buda side of the river by a pilework bridge. King Béla IV (1235–70) had several religious orders settle here including Dominican nuns, to whom he entrusted his beloved daughter, Margit (Margaret). The romantic ruins and also the island's name both date from that time. By way of contrast, it was here too that the Turkish pasha entrusted the ladies from his harem to eunuchs; this 'island of women' thus developed quite a legendary reputation in Christian Europe.

'Palatin' archduke Joseph used the island as a summer residence and had the Botanical Garden laid out in 1796. However, the devastating floods of 1836 washed away any magnificence there may have been. His son Rudolf restored the Roman tradition of the thermal bath, and the 'Palatinus' thermal baths on the western arm of the Danube

Island service

were named in honour of both of them. The open-air theatre beneath the huge water-tower here provides evening entertainment; superb opera and concert performances have regularly taken place here ever since 1937. After World War I, the short-lived Soviet republic allowed 'ordinary' people free access to the island as well, and the people of Budapest were quick to seize the opportunity. However, very few can afford the luxury of dining in the elegant garden restaurant of the **Grand Hotel Ramada**.

An extra number 26 bus to the island, with an open top, runs at weekends, and stops at all the island's major landmarks, while down by the fountains in the southern part there are two establishments renting out go-karts. The central part of the island is a well tended park, with a network of broad footpaths. On the western side, the open-air **Palatinus Thermal Baths** are just the place for a relaxing swim, and the island bus stops there, too. The new building containing the Thermal Hotel towers above the island's northeastern point, and the stylish **Grand Hotel** next door to it, with its magnificent restaurant and café, is highly recommended.

Option 7. Along Andrássy út

A stroll along Andrássy út to the Millennium Monument, on Hero's Square, with two fine art galleries. Then a meal in the City Park at the world-famous Gundel restaurant, and a ride back home on continental Europe's oldest underground railway.

– All Metro lines: get off at Deák tér –

St Stephen's Basilica

This itinerary begins at Vörösmarty tér. Walk past the **Luxus** department store and down Deák Ferenc utca, where the superb **Kempinski** hotel opened in 1992. The Protestant Church on Deák tér is almost spartan in comparison.

Deák tér is actually one of the busiest squares in all of Budapest, not least because all three of the city's Metro lines intersect here. Now head off in the direction of Erzsébet tér, the neighbouring square, passing the bus station and heading towards the towers of the Neo-Romanesque **St Stephen's Basilica**. Everybody calls it a 'basilica' even though the architecture isn't exactly reminiscent of Roman models. Dur-

The Opera House dates from 1884, and inspired Mahler and Puccini

ing its construction in 1868, the mighty dome, almost 100m (330ft) high, collapsed because of faulty structural planning, and so it was only as recently as 1906 that this church, which has room for almost 9,000 people, could finally be consecrated. A steady stream of Hungarian Catholics make the pilgrimage to see the right hand of St Stephen, a relic here with a chapel all to itself.

After this brief detour turn into **Andrássy út**; Hungarian prime minister Andrássy gave the go-ahead for its construction in 1868. After the advantageous Compromise with Austria had been reached, many felt that the time had finally come for the town planners' vision of a proper connection between the City Park and the Chain Bridge to be turned into reality. What was more, the country's 'thousand-year celebrations' were drawing nigh, and so the plan was to mark the event by unveiling a heroic statue at the end of the new road. By 1886, a full ten years before the event, the new road – apart from the odd gap – had been largely completed. Even today, its buildings still convey a strong stylistic unity.

The lower section of the street is really narrow, but the tree-shaded pavements here are still a good place for a stroll. This area is notable for its specialised shops. Soon you'll come to the **Opera House** on your left, an impressive building dating from 1884. The facade is richly ornamented, and the building can house an audience of 1,300 beneath its broad dome. Music history was written here: Gustav Mahler made his youthful debut here as chief conductor, Puccini personally supervised the first performance of *Madame Butterfly*, and from 1947–50 Otto Klemperer brought the Opera House international fame once again. The daytime box office on the left-hand side of the building (open 10am–7pm) may have tickets, but it's usually safer to order in advance from the central ticket office at Andrássy út 18.

Opposite the Opera House is the **School of Ballet**, housed in the Palais Drechsler, which was built by Ödön Lechner. Lechner, who became famous as an exponent of Art Nouveau, kept modestly to the guidelines of Opera House architect Miklós Ybl, creating a purely neoclassical building.

Fresco in the Academy of Music

Nagymező utca crosses behind the Opera House. Because of its cinemas, theatres and nightclubs it is jokingly referred to by the locals as 'Broadway'. Nearby is the stylish coffee-house called **Muvési** at Andrassy út 29, where Budapest's Bohemian contingent gathers early on weekday mornings.

Liszt tér – for some strange reason – contains a statue of Endry Ady, a poet; another poet, Mór Jókai, is similarly immortalised in stone on the other side of the street. Franz Liszt, the great Hungarian musician who actually hardly spoke a word of the language after a career in France, Austria and Germany, has not been forgotten however: the **Academy of Music** behind the square was named after him, and a bit further on, at Andrássy út 67, his former apartment has been converted into a **Liszt Museum**.

The **Octagon** was created by the architect Antal Skalniczky; the Outer Ring Road (known as Teréz körút) runs straight through the middle of it. After the Octagon the Andrássy út gets wider. The **Lukács** coffee-house on the left here is a good place for a break; the magnificent hall on the first floor has made the place a listed building.

The splendour of the apartments around the **Kodály körönd** (circular flower-bed), has faded, but the shady beer-garden on the left-hand side is still a nice place to sit. Further on the street widens, as front gardens start appearing in front of the various facades. There

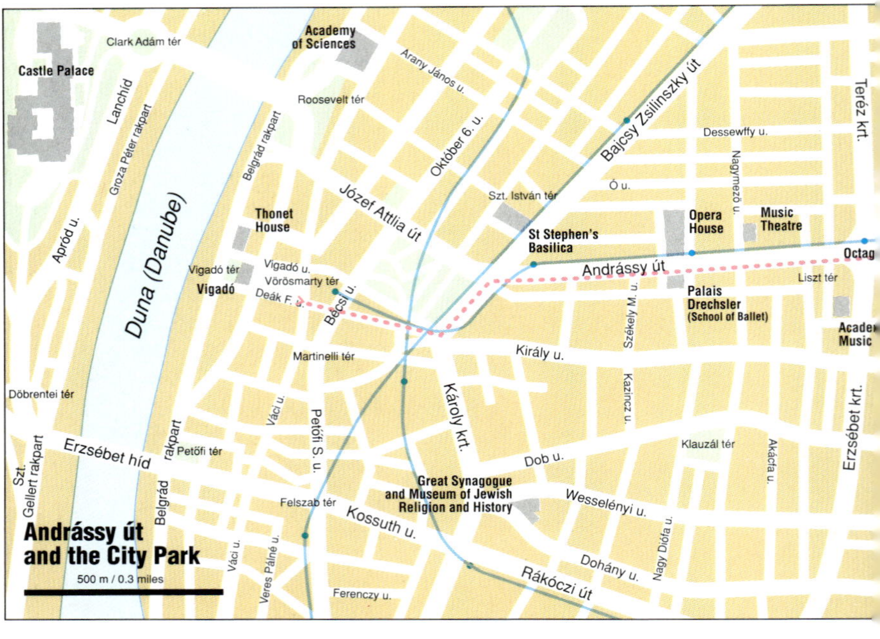

Andrássy út and the City Park

500 m / 0.3 miles

are several fine Neo-Renaissance and Secessionist-style villas here, while the interesting-looking 3-star **Central** hotel is almost Cubist.

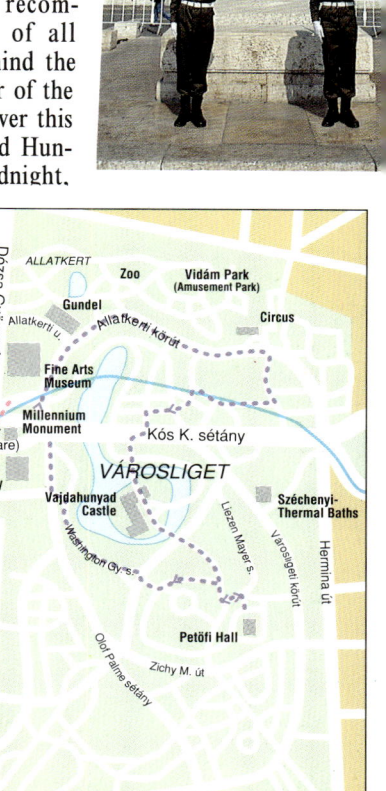

Continue to the end of the avenue where Hero's Square is dominated by the **Millennium Monument**, erected in 1896 for the 'thousand-year celebration of the Magyar conquest'. At the top of the high column the archangel Gabriel hands his crown to King Stephen I, the founder of the state, in exact accordance with the myth of the country's foundation. Immortalised in stone at the foot of the statue are the seven legendary tribal chieftains who took part in the original Magyar conquest. This huge monument to Hungarian national pride is flanked by two colonnades with allegorical depictions of war and peace and statues of national heroes.

The enormous square is flanked by two museums. The **Art Gallery** on the right was first opened in 1896, and for many years was a stubborn opponent of everything modern and/or offensive in Hungarian art. All that has radically altered and the gallery today features some fascinating exhibitions, films and performances. The monumental **Fine Arts Museum** opposite, from its Ancient Egypt department all the way to its 20th-century paintings, provides an impressive documentation of art history.

Three restaurants nearby are highly recommended: the traditional **Gundel** first of all (Allartkerti körút 2, Tel: 122 1002), behind the museum on the left. Janos Gundel, founder of the legendary dynasty of famous cooks, took over this building in 1910. His son Károly invented Hungarian *nouvelle cuisine*. From noon till midnight, exquisite delicacies are served here, in the magnificent garden or the dignified dining-room. A classic Gundel menu dating from 1912 begins with *palatsch* soup, followed by zander *à la maison*. The recommended main course is *fricassée* of beef on mimosa salad, with *Crêpes à la Gundel* to finish off. Today the same meal costs around 3,000 forints; the menus up on display in the old foyer reveal that prices were just a little lower in the old days.

Another marvellous place to eat is the **Robinson** directly opposite (Allartkerti körút, right next to the lake). The restaurant terrace almost seems to be hovering above the lake in the City Park, and there are also several tables in the stylish pavilion.

The **Taverna** restaurant, at the end of Andrássy út, is a lot more down-to-earth altogether. This inexpensive restaurant is inside a remarkably beautiful house dating from the turn of the century. Food is also served out in the garden, in the shade of the old plane trees.

Right outside the front door of the 'Taverna' lies the entrance to the **oldest underground line** in continental Europe, which was opened in 1896 for the country's thousand-year anniversary celebrations. Take the M1 back to Deák tér, where the other two lines intersect, or to the terminus at Vörösmarty tér. Anyone keener on staying above ground can take a No 1 bus which in daytime runs every five minutes to Deák tér, then on to the Astoria.

Option 8. City Park

This large park offers attractions for young and old alike, including a zoo, a romantic castle and a nostalgic thermal bath.

– Metro M1: get off at Hósök tere –

A big attraction

Budapest's small but enchanting **zoo** (open daily 10am–3pm, during summer 9am–6pm), with its Art Nouveau animal houses, can be found on the left after the museum and the Gundel. If you then follow along the perimeter wall of the zoo you'll come to the domed **circus** building and the **amusement park**; its quaint attractions, including the big wheel and the big dipper, only operate from April to September however. There again, the huge **Széchenyi Thermal Baths** are open all year round. Built for medicinal purposes at the beginning of this century, the baths were extended once again in 1927 to accommodate the general public. In the warm-water pools (27°C/80°F and 38°C/100°F) you can see the local chess stars playing on floating cork boards. There are games galore

Relaxed concentration in the Széchenyi Thermal Baths

in the park next door too: groups of onlookers cluster round games of rummy and bridge, table-tennis balls and shuttlecocks hurtle through the air, and near the pond children can be seen practising somersaults on a trampoline, normally under the watchful eye of a sports trainer.

Vajdahunyad Castle

On the island in the pond lies **Vajdahunyad Castle**, in part a reconstruction of the castle of the same name in Transylvania. This highly imaginative and nostalgic building, the work of architect Ignác Alpár, was originally constructed out of papier-mâché for the thousand-year celebration, and was so popular with the people of Budapest that it was reconstructed again in 1904 out of stone.

The eastern part of the park contains several other interesting buildings; young people in particular should make sure they visit the **Petőfi Hall**, a very popular – and very loud – disco. Friday night is Oldies Night (people that is, not records).

Option 9. Jewish Budapest

A visit to the quarter of the city beyond the Inner Ring Road and north of Rákóczi út, with its small Jewish community. Behind the Great Synagogue in the Erzsébetváros district there are several interesting arts and crafts shops, and also some kosher restaurants with exceptionally friendly service.

– Metro M2: get off at Astoria –

From very early on, Budapest's Jews made a huge contribution to the city's development. At the end of the last century more than one quarter of the population of the city was Jewish. Jews were accepted as Hungarians of Jewish faith, and were never placed into ghettoes. Only under the Horthy regime, and especially

The new generation

Hebrew on the Great Synagogue

under German and Hungarian Nazi rule was this unquestioned harmony shattered. Only around 10,000 Jews now live in Hungary, most of them in Budapest.

The **Great Synagogue** at Dohány utca 2–8, just one block north of the intersection of Kossuth Lajos utca and Károly körút, is the centre of the Jewish community. Built between 1854 and 1859 in Byzantine-Moorish style, with its striking onion domes, the synagogue accommodates up to 3,000 worshippers. Behind the magnificent rose-windowed facade, the interior is divided up into three aisles; the men use the ground floor, and the women the balustrades. The smaller synagogue in the same complex seats around 250, and is used by the community for daily services. It was built in 1931 and is consecrated to 'the heroes of the resistance'.

In the adjoining courtyard of honour, in front of the **Jewish Museum**, stands Imre Varga's *Weeping Willow*, with the names of thousands of victims of Fascism engraved into its leaves. The newly-renovated building and its collection can be visited on weekdays, 10am–1pm (outside 'service' hours), and concerts are also given now and then on the synagogue's magnificent organ.

The section of the city to the east is called Erzsébetváros, and is still distinctively Jewish. One block north of the synagogue is the Dob utca with all its churches, antique shops, bookstores and craft shops, and it leads to the main square, **Klauzál tér**. Here, the pleasant **Carmel** restaurant serves up kosher meals for the Jewish community; the waiters, fluent in English and German, happily advise on the selection of delicious and inexpensive dishes.

The 'Weeping Willow' by Imre Varga

Activities

It has often been said that Budapest is a bridge between East and West, but it is only by immersing yourself in some of the city's very special attractions that you'll discover just how far this is true.

Budapest, marked by centuries of struggle between the Habsburgs and the Ottomans, between the Catholic West and Islamic East, is quite unique in that it retains a happy mixture of both cultures in its everyday life. This is most obvious when you're lying back enjoying a Turkish bath, or indulging in the nostalgic atmosphere of the city's coffee-houses, many of which easily rival those in Vienna.

A cultural experience

Baths

Budapest has 30 different baths, with many fed by thermal springs. Some have been popular since Roman times. Here is a selection:

KIRALY BATHS
Fő utca 82–86 (in Víziváros, red line M2: Batthyány tér)
Opening times: Monday–Saturday 7am–7pm, Sunday 7am–1pm.
Separate opening times for genders; Women: Tuesday, Thursday, Saturday and Sunday; Men: Monday, Wednesday and Friday.

LUKACS ÉS USZODA BATHS
Frankel Leó utca 25-29 (north part of Víziváros in direction of Óbuda, red line M2: Batthyány tér)
Opening times: Monday–Saturday 6am–8pm, Sunday 6am–6pm.
Turkish baths dating back to the 16th century with a fine foyer.

RUDAS BATHS
Döbrentei tér 9 (trams No 9, 18, 19 and also from Pest No 47 and 49)
Opening times: Monday–Friday 6am–6pm, Saturday and Sunday 6am–noon. The baths, with their red marble decor and slightly radioactive spa water, were opened by Pasha Mustafa Sokoli in 1566.

GELLÉRT BATHS AND OPEN-AIR POOL

Kelenhegyi út 4 (southern part of the Buda side by the Freedom Bridge, trams No 9, 18, 19, and from Pest No 47 and 49)
Opening times: Monday–Saturday 6am–8pm, Sunday 6am–4pm. In Art Deco style with a large pool and Turkish steam baths; in summer several open-air pools are available (*see Day 3*).

Many coffee-houses are still as elegant as they used to be

PALATINUS BEACH

Margaret Island (bus No 26)
Opening times: daily 7am–7pm, mid-April until end of October only. Open-air baths with thermal pool; part of a large complex containing 7 pools including a wave pool, sauna, children's playgrounds and also a café.

Coffee-houses

The gallant, old-fashioned Viennese greeting *küss die Hand', schöne Frau* ('kiss your hand, beautiful lady') has its equivalent here in Budapest too: *kezét csókolom!* It's a cliché that's survived the changes of the past few decades, and is still not out of place in the city's coffee-houses. It's all still there: the elegant ladies with their cigarette-holders and extravagant-looking hats, gentlemen buried in their newspapers giving the odd sign of life with a puff of smoke, and the multilingual waitress with her lace bonnet, lace-up shoes and even more tightly-laced corset. An even more special feature of Budapest cafés is that the cakes and sweets are usually produced on the premises. There's always a huge selection in the display windows of these coffee-houses, known as *Cukrászda: sós és édes teasütémeny* (savoury or sweet pastries). Equally delicious are a dozen variations of *torta* and *beigli* (small pastries filled with meat or nuts). Here is a selection of the finest traditional cafés in Budapest:

RUSZWURM

Szentháromság u. 7
Open daily 10am–8pm
News of this wonderfully intimate café, only a few steps away from the Matthias Church on Castle Hill, had spread to Vienna as long ago as the turn of the century. The inexpensive iced coffees and strudels are just as popular today with locals and visitors alike.

ANGELIKA

Batthyány tér 7 (M2), in Víziváros
Open daily 10am–8pm
A tastefully furnished, old-fashioned café on the Buda side. Lots of space but the niches are nice and intimate, and the delicious cakes and sweets are made on the premises.

AUGUSZT

Fény u. 8, on the Buda side
Open daily 9am–9pm
Rather hidden away, just a few steps from busy Moszkva tér (M2). Privately owned; 1930s atmosphere skilfully maintained. The ice-cream cakes are particularly good.

MŰVÉSZ

Andrássy út 29 (M1 Opera station)
Open daily 8am–9pm
The artist's café *par excellence*, in the cultural section of Pest. Bleary-eyed alternatives gather here, particularly after long nights in clubs. Specialities include candied fruits and marzipan pastries.

GERBEAUD

Vörösmarty tér 7 (M1 terminus)
Open daily 9am–9pm
A spacious coffee-house with a summer terrace, and the most pleasant place for a rendezvous in all of Pest. There are always a couple of chairs free. Broad selection of specialities, both large and small.

LUKACS

Andrássy út 70 (M1
Kodály körönd station)
Open daily 8am–9pm
A subsidiary of the famous Gerbeaud on Vörösmarty tér but far less crowded, and worth a visit if only for its superb interior.

NEW YORK

Erzsébet körút 9–11 (M2 station: Blaha L. tér)
Open daily 9am–midnight
A very fine coffee-house and restaurant on the Outer Ring, halfway between Andrássy út and Rákóczi út. Much past splendour, and a lovingly restored interior.

The City's Museums

I've already mentioned quite a few of the museums in the various full-day and half-day itineraries. Here is a selection of the most important museums, arranged region by region.

Museums in Budapest are generally open daily except Monday 10am–6pm. Even though entrance prices were increased recently, they are still remarkably low by Western standards (20–100Ft.). On one day every week – usually on Tuesday – entry to all the museums in Hungary is free of charge.

Information on special exhibitions is available from 'Tourinform', Tel: 117 9800.

The Museum of Fine Arts

Cake mosaic at the Kereskedelmi

On Castle Hill

NEMZETI GALÉRIA
(National Gallery)
Royal Palace, wings B, C and D.
Tel: 175 7533
On the ground floor, a medieval lapidary and also a collection of Gothic sculptures and paintings. On the first floor, Late Gothic art, including the magnificent panel *The Visitation of Mary and Elisabeth* by an anonymous master. Beyond it, up on the second floor, the work of Hungarian painters and sculptors can be admired. Alongside much historic painting there are works by Mihály Munkácsy, Szinyei Merse and Miklós Izsó.

BUDAPESTI TÖRTÉNE MUZEUM (History Museum)
Royal Palace, wing A. Tel: 175 7533
Archaeological finds covering the city's 2,000-year history. Medieval relics and Gothic sculptures are among the exhibits.

LEGUJABBKORI TÖRTÉNETI MUZEUM (Museum of Modern History)
Royal Palace, wing A. Tel: 175 7533
History of the Workers' Movement and of everyday culture in Budapest. Extensive collection of historic photographs.

KERESKEDELMI ÉS VENDÉGLATOIPARI MUZEUM
(Museum of Trade and Commerce)
Fortuna utca 4, near Royal Palace. Tel: 175 6249
The women attendants here also speak English and German and are happy to provide a commentary, creating a lively introduction to Hungarian industrial and cultural history since the middle of the last century.

In Óbuda

IMRE VARGA MUZEUM
Laktanya utca 7, HÉV station: Arpád híd. Tel: 180 3274
Varga is probably the most famous modern Hungarian artist still alive. Although he did enjoy official recognition under the Communist regime and represented his country at the Venice Film Festival in 1984, he has never allowed himself to be compromised politically. His sculptures on display in the museum, with their overtly anti-militaristic and anti-jingoistic slant, make this clear.

VASARHELYI MUZEUM
Szentélek tér 6, HÉV station: Arpád híd. Tel: 184 0540
This museum, housed in the former Zichy castle, mostly contains
the early works of Vásárhelyí, who was the founder of Op Art (the
art of optical illusion).

LAJOS KASSAK MUZEUM
Fő tér 1, HÉV station: Arpád híd. Tel: 168 7021
This anarchical genius – a writer, sculptor and arts organiser – has
been neglected far too long. The museum contains wonderful cata-
logues and brochures, also dealing with Kassák's contemporaries.
Concerts are held occasionally in the main hall and the courtyard
during the summer season.

Aquincum

AQUINCUMI MUZEUM
*Szentendrei út 139, suburban railway HÉV from Batthyány tér – sta-
tion: 'Aquincum'. Tel: 180 4650*
Open daily except Monday 10am–5pm, 15 April to end-October.
The Roman town of *Aquincum*, which had a population of around
50,000 in its heyday, has had a quarter of its remains excavated.
The rectangular street grid with sewers and waterways, and public
baths and market halls can all be clearly made out. Statues and
tombstones from the site can be seen in a columned hall surrounding the museum, which itself is very extensive.

Exhibits include a water organ created in the 3rd century, repro-
ductions true to scale and a series of everyday objects, including
coins and cult artefacts. The real highlight of the museum, however,
is a large statue of Mithras.

In Pest

NÉPRAJZI MUZEUM (Ethnographic Museum)
Kossuth Lajos tér 12, M2 station: K.L. tér.
Tel: 132 6349
A fine building, formerly the supreme court of justice and with wonderful frescos, contains a magnificent collection dealing with the history and
culture of the people of Hungary, particularly fo-
cusing on Magyar folk art.

LISZT FERENC EMLÉKMUZEUM (Franz Liszt Museum)
Vörösmarty utca 35, corner Andrássy út, M1 station:
V. utca. Tel: 122 9804
Open Monday–Friday noon–5pm, Saturday
9am–1pm, closed Sunday. A museum celebrating
the composer in Liszt's former apartment, with in-
struments and furniture.

Encounter in Mücsarnok

SZEPMÜVÉSZETI MUZEUM (Fine Arts)
Hősök tere, M1 station: H. tere, Tel: 142 9759
Fine arts from abroad. Of particular note is the gallery of Italian
Renaissance masters, and also Flemish genre painters.

MÜCSARNOK (Art Gallery)
Hősök tere, M1 station: H. tere, Tel: 122 7405
Alternating exhibitions featuring modern art both local and foreign. Performances, events and film shows in the Art-Cinema. Cat-
alogues and art posters on sale. Check before you go, though; it has
been closed recently for renovation.

KÖZLEKEDÉSI MUZEUM (Transport Museum)
*Városligeti krt. 11, in the City Park next to the Petőfi Hall, terminus
of the M1 – Mexicói út. Tel: 142 0565*
The history of aviation, rail travel, seafaring and motoring in Hungary, documented very attractively by means of original models and
a large amount of photographs.

ZSIDO MUZEUM (Jewish Museum)
Dohány u. 2, same building as Great Synagogue, M2 station: Astoria
Open Monday and Thursday 2–6pm, Tuesday and Friday
10am–1pm. The history of the Jews of Hungary; many documents
and photographs.

NEMZETI MUZEUM (National Museum)
Múzeum körút 14–16, M3 station: Kálvin tér. Tel: 133 4400
The history of the Magyars, from their emigration from Central
Siberia to the Austro-Hungarian monarchy.

IPARMÜVÉSZETI MUZEUM (Museum of Arts and Crafts)
*Ülloi út 33, in the south-eastern part of Pest, M3 station: Ferenc
körút. Tel: 117 5635 and 117 5222*
Built in Art Deco style in 1896, this building contains two permanent arts and crafts exhibitions dealing with the history of European styles, and also has a well-stocked textile section containing
oriental carpets and Flemish tapestries.

The National Museum

EXCURSIONS

Hungary is a small place, and all kinds of interesting destinations can be reached in a few hours by car or by train from Budapest.

Magnificent Lake Balaton, situated in the southwest of the country, where you can combine sailing and swimming activities with visits to several historic little towns around the lake, is a three-hour-long trip by motorway, or by rail from Budapest's South Station.

Just as close is the rural town of Kecskemét in the southeast. Magnificent Art Deco houses and numerous concerts and folk festivals reflect the strong cultural traditions of Hungary's rural population. Kecskemét is also the gateway to the legendary Puszta, which has largely retained its stark beauty despite Rural Hungary tourism.

Szentendre

The shortest and also the most attractive excursion from Budapest takes you north, however, to the romantic landscape around the Danube Bend. The Serbian enclave of **Szentendre**, the legendary **Visegrád** and the cathedral town of **Esztergom** are very easy to reach by train, car and even by bicycle.

The nicest way to organise this excursion is to combine it with a cruise up the Danube on a steamer, because you can relax on deck and enjoy the view of the city panorama and the magnificent meadows along the banks. In season, cheap boat trips run regularly from the quay down in front of the **Vigadó** as far as Esztergom.

Of course it's even easier to book yourself into a day trip, of the type organised by IBUSZ and other agencies. For 4,000Ft. you go on a morning trip up the west bank of the Danube to Szentendre, on an old-fashioned steamer. After a two-hour stopover, featuring a stroll around this romantic little town and a coffee break, you then travel on to **Visegrád**, where a bus will be waiting to transport you up to the medieval castle. The exciting trip back, this time with the current, takes you along the eastern bank of the Danube, and by mid-afternoon you're back in the city centre. The guided tour, run by a guide fluent in both English and German, and an acceptable meal with wine on board the steamer are also included in the overall price.

Szentendre is the centre of Serbian settlement in Hungary. The Serbs arrived here as long ago as 1389 after losing a battle to the Turks, and more refugees followed their patriarch Crnojewic around 1690. Four of the seven churches in this small town still have Orthodox congregations. In 1763, Serbian merchants also footed the bill for the **Plague Cross** in the central square, **Fő tér**.

Szentendre

In May and June this intimate little square turns into a stage with spectators for the theatre and opera festival here, which is gaining more fame with every year that passes. The surrounding buildings are also included in the event, such as the balconies on the Church of the Annunciation and the former Serbian high school. Today the latter houses the **Local History Museum**, containing a fine collection of Hungarian and Serbian folkwear.

A winding street leads away from the square up to **Templon tér**. A fortified village stood on this site as long ago as the 12th century; today the plateau is dominated by the Catholic parish church, which despite baroque additions still retains several visible traces of its medieval heritage.

The most striking church tower in town is that of the so-called **Belgrade Cathedral**, the episcopal church of the Orthodox patriarch. Magnificently renovated, its bright red and white colours stand out against the town.

Atmospheric surroundings like this stimulate the creative imagination, and Szentendre has also gained fame for its artists' colony. **Margit Kovács**, a potter, who died in 1977, was one of its leading lights; her highly expressive work can be admired in a special museum at György utca 1. Dozens of shops here sell all kinds of arts and crafts, and antiques fans will also find a great deal of interesting artefacts.

There's a fine view from Visegrád castle

Visegrád

Visegrád, the 'high castle', was once famous throughout Europe for the magnificent Renaissance palazzo that King Mátyás had completed there towards the end of the 15th century. Unfortunately, little remains of the splendour of this focal point of European culture and politics. Destruction wrought by wars and landslides has left only the reconstructed arcades of the inner courtyard. The fortress-like **castle** towers over this village, which played a historical role yet again in 1991 when the heads of state from Hungary, Czechoslovakia and Poland met here to sign a cooperation agreement. A path leads up to the castle; a more comfortable way up, though, is to take the bus up the panoramic road. From the battlements of the castle, which has been turned into a museum of local history, there is a magnificent view of the Danube valley. To the north you can also make out the unfinished **Nagymaros dam**, a bone of contention at present between the Slovaks – who want to carry on building it at all costs in order to turn Bratislava into a free trade zone and a Danube port – and the Hungarians. Its construction has brought ecological and economic interests face to face.

Esztergom

Esztergom, roughly 60km (37 miles) upriver, is the traditional seat of the primate of the Catholic Church in Hungary. Once again it was King Mátyás who turned this town into the cultural and spiritual centre of his empire, and once again, it was wars that destroyed most of the magnificent Renaissance buildings which once stood here. The town, which is actually quite attractive, is thus dominated by the enormous **Basilica**, which was consecrated in 1856. Just about the only remarkable thing about this building, however, is that Franz Liszt composed his **Gran Mass** in honour of its consecration (Gran was the name given to Esztergom under the

Austrians), and that the charming 16th-century **Bagócz Chapel** has been preserved intact beneath its mighty 100-metre (330-ft) high dome.

Esztergom

Eating Out

As far as food and drink are concerned, Budapest is in the same situation as many other aspects of the country's culture: not a lot is originally Hungarian, because the nomadic Magyars had very little spare time to sit back and indulge in gourmet snacks and viniculture.

It was only when they settled in the Danube valley that the Magyars first discovered the subtler aspects of food and drink, and they went on to adopt several specialities from the Italians, the French, the Serbs and the Turks, finally using some genuine Hungarian imagination to concoct some utterly delicious recipes. The restaurants of Budapest today thus feature such dishes as the aromatic and very Turkish *Loin of Pork Gül Baba style*, the very Austrian and very filling *Chicken Pörkölt with Letscho and sour cream*, and the refined French *Wild Boar Steak in Calvados Sauce*.

Hungarian wines, too, have developed from simple *vins ordinaires* to very fine wines with excellent bouquets. That applies not only to the Tokay wines from the volcanic soil around Balaton, but also to the country's dry Rieslings and to the very strong *Bikavér* ('Bull's Blood'). A good, well-matured wine is marked *puttonyos*; eight points indicates the highest quality, and from four upwards it's certainly worth giving the wine in question a quick taste. Other important descriptions to look out for are *száras* (dry), *félszáras*

Hungarian Cuisine ... a little bit of everything

(medium dry) and *édes* (sweet). Below is a list of restaurants and wine bars where the food and drink is particularly delicious:

PEST-BUDA
Fortuna utca 3, Tel: 122 3849
Open daily 5pm–midnight, Sunday open for lunch too. On Castle Hill, just a few steps away from the Mátyás Church.
A pleasant restaurant with traditional cuisine. Friendly, attentive staff and a fine interior will enhance your meal.

ALABARDOS
Országház utca 2, Tel: 156 0851
Open Monday–Saturday 6pm–midnight, and also for lunch during peak season. Closed Sunday. On Castle Hill, directly opposite the Mátyás Church.
Three very different interiors in which to dine: rustic in the cellar, elegant on the ground floor and generous on the terrace leading to the large inner courtyard. The restaurant is extremely well-situated, and this is reflected in the prices.

KACSA
Fő utca 75, Tel: 135 3357
Open daily 6pm–4am. In Víziváros opposite the Király Baths, red M2 station: Batthyány tér.
Small, but excellent establishment with a few very well-selected specialities, attentive service and agreeable piano music.

KIS-BUDA
Frankel Leó utca 34, Tel: 115 2244
Open daily noon–midnight, Sunday for lunch only. In the northern part of Víziváros, red M2 station: Batthyány tér.
An unassuming inn (*vendéglő*) on the outside, the Kis-Buda is actually a

gourmet restaurant that also keeps up the Turkish traditions of this area of the city.

KISBUDA GYÖNGYE
Kenyeres utca 34, Tel: 168 6402
Open daily noon–midnight, Sunday lunchtime only. In Óbuda, HÉV station: Florian tér.
Stylish subsidiary of the Kis-Buda, with traditional and imaginative dishes jostling for diners' attention on the menu.

SIPOS HALASZKERT
Fő tér 6, Tel: 188 8745
Open daily noon–midnight, bar stays open till 4am. On the old market square of Óbuda, HÉV station: Florian tér.
A traditional seafood restaurant, which also does excellent meat dishes. Traditional decor and tasty food, and in summer chairs are placed outside in the quiet inner courtyard.

Hot stuff

SZAZÉVES
Pesti Barnabás utca 2, Tel: 118 3608
Open daily noon–midnight. On the
Pest side of the Elisabeth Bridge, blue
line M3 station: Felszabulás tér.
The oldest restaurant in Pest; its history is documented for visitors. The menu is very attractive indeed, not least because of the amazingly good value. In summer there's a fine shady garden to sit in.

GUNDEL
Állartkerti körút 2, Tel: 122 1002 and
121 3550
Open daily from noon–midnight, hot
food noon–4pm and 7pm–midnight.
At the end of Andrássy út, M1 station:
Hósök tere.
This is the Hungarian *nouvelle cuisine* restaurant *par excellence*; it has been run by top chef Janos Gundel and his descendants since 1910. Wonderful rooms and a magnificent terrace, where the sound of elephants trumpeting can sometimes be heard from the zoo nearby. Since expectations here are usually as high as the prices, you may experience the odd disappointment.

Dried chillies

ROBINSON
Allartkerti körút, Tel: 118 7634
Open daily noon–3pm and 6pm–midnight. Great location next to the lake
in the City Park, yellow line M1 station: Hósök tere.
The magnificent setting and the superb food make up for the high prices here. Also a very fine coffee-house.

NEW YORK (HUNGARIA)
Erzsébet körút 9–11, Tel: 122 3849
Open daily noon–midnight. On the
Outer Ring Road north of the red line
M2 station: Blaha L. tér.
The ultimate nostalgic café-restaurant, which has been recently restored at great expense.

NAUTILUS
Váci utca 72, Tel: 138 4830
Open daily noon–2am. M3 station:
Kálvin tér.
Superb seafood, but also very delicious game and poultry specialities, all at very reasonable prices.

VEGETARIUM RESTAURANT
Cukor utca 3, Tel: 138 3710
Open daily noon–10pm. Blue line M3
station: Felszabadulás tér.
One of the few vegetarian restaurants in Budapest.

Also recommended for vegetarians are the city's Chinese and Thai restaurants, for example:

TAIWAN RESTAURANT
Gyáli út 3/b, Tel: 133 1236
Open daily noon–1am. Near the blue
line M3 station: Nagyvárad tér in the
southeastern part of Pest.
Excellent Chinese cuisine at low prices.

Shopping

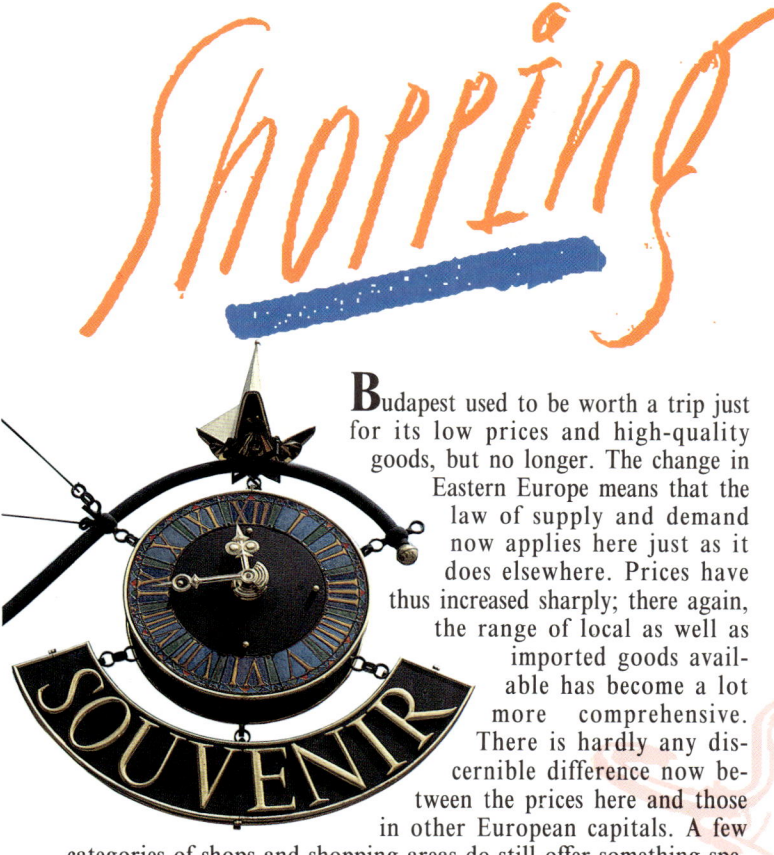

Budapest used to be worth a trip just for its low prices and high-quality goods, but no longer. The change in Eastern Europe means that the law of supply and demand now applies here just as it does elsewhere. Prices have thus increased sharply; there again, the range of local as well as imported goods available has become a lot more comprehensive. There is hardly any discernible difference now between the prices here and those in other European capitals. A few categories of shops and shopping areas do still offer something special, though, and we list them below:

Secondhand Bookshops

Everyone keen on rummaging through old shelves and peering at old etchings will have no problem finding things to do in Budapest. Remember, though, that antiques which are more than 50 years old may not be taken out of the country. Special permits can be organised via the respective dealers, but the process tends to take quite a while. Opening times: Monday–Friday 10am–6pm, Sunday 10am–1pm.

OWL ANTIKVARIUM
Váci utca 28 (M3 Felszabadulás tér.)
Tel: 117 4924
Hungarian and foreign-language rarities, with competent advice given in German and English too.

BUDAI KRONIKA ANTIKVARIUM
Várfok u. 8 (M2 Moszkva tér.)
Tel: 135 2168
A particularly fine assortment of etchings and engravings.

BUDAVAR ANTIKVARIUM
Országház u. 8 (on Castle Hill)
Tel: 156 0428
Lots of postcards and old albums.

CENTRAL ANTIKVARIUM
Múzeum körút 13–5 (M2 Astoria)
Tel: 117 3514
Opposite the National Museum. Broad selection of Hungarian and foreign-language books, postcards and engravings. An in-house auction is held on the last Saturday in every month.

HONTERUS
Múzeum körút 3 (M2 Astoria)
Tel: 117 3270
Directly opposite the National Museum. German-language literature, magazines and postcards.

BORDA
Balzac u. 50/a (M3 Nyugati pu.)
Tel: 149 9279
Open Monday–Friday 10am–1pm and 4–7pm, Saturday 10am–2pm. Specialist literature and unusual titles.

BIBLIOTHEKA
Andrássy út 2 (all Metro lines: Deák tér)
Tel: 131 5132
Specialises in old maps and engravings.

HUNNIA
József körút 59–61 (M2 Blaha L. tér)
Tel: 134 1458
Large selection of books.

ANTIKVARIUM – MUSIC ANTIQUES
Múzeum körút 17–21 (M2 Astoria)
Tel: 117 4978
Sheet music, records and rarities.

OFOTÉRT – ANTIQUE PHOTOS
Alpári Gyula u. 2 (all Metro lines: Deák tér)
Tel: 117 2341
Open Monday–Friday 10am–6pm. Antique photographic equipment, optical articles, gramophones, counting machines, historically interesting photographs.

Bookshops

Despite the recent massive price rises, books in Hungary are still a lot cheaper than they are in Western Europe, and even imported books cost only 60 percent of their sale price in, say, Germany. The same applies to records, CDs, videos and tapes; there again, quite a few pirated copies are also on sale.

LITÉA
Hess András tér
Tel: 175 4385
An exceptionally attractive bookshop with a small tea-house in a rear courtyard, not far from the Mátyás Church. Large selection of travel guides and foreign-language literature.

KOSSMUTH BOOKSHOP
Vörösmarty tér 4 (M1 Vörösmarty tér.)
Tel: 118 3674
Publications both domestic and imported, art books, slides.

KÖNYVESHAZ BOOKSHOP
Váci út 19 (M1 Vörösmarty tér.)
Tel: 149 8320
The largest bookshop in Hungary, with its sales rooms in a former factory floor. Books at reduced prices.

CORVINA – BOOKS AND MUSIC
Kossuth Lajos út 4 (M2 Astoria)
Tel: 118 3603
The most important foreign-language publishers in Hungary (Corvina) have their headquarters here. Art books,

Plenty to read

travel books, language books and cassettes, records and CDs.

FERENC ERKEL – BOOK AND MUSIC SHOP
Erszébet körút 52 (M3 Nyugati pu.)
Tel: 122 8206
A good assortment of foreign-language art and travel books, and also cassettes, records, CDs, videos and sheet music.

WRITERS' BOOKSHOP
Andrássy út (M1 Oktogon)
Spacious bookstore specialising in Hungarian literature. Comfy corners to sit and browse in.

Antiques Shops
Although the era of bargains is long gone in this sector as well, you may still be lucky enough to find the odd gem because money is at a premium in Hungary at the moment, and many of the locals are selling off their possessions. Also, do remember that it is forbidden to remove any antique more than 50 years old from the country unless you get a special permit. It's only the proper dealers who'll inform you of this – and they're the only people you should buy from.
Opening times of antiques shops are generally Monday–Friday 10am–6pm, Saturday 10am–1pm, and sometimes Sunday as well.

RELIKVIA
Fortuna u. 14 (on Castle Hill)
Tel: 175 6971
Nostalgic knick-knacks, clothes, dolls, old cameras, as well as the usual furniture, glass and porcelain.

PARTI ANTIQUITAS
Országház u. 2 (on Castle Hill)
Tel: 175 0480
Glassware, porcelain, dolls, furniture.

ANTIQUITIES
Váci utca 66 (M3 Felszabadulás tér.)
Tel: 118 7417
Tucked away in a basement, this shop has a superb assortment of old furniture, mirrors, dolls and carpets. The friendly lady who owns it speaks excellent English as well as German and will give you expert advice.

BAV
Various different shops all belonging to a chain of department stores. You may be lucky enough to find the odd bargain here, but you can also very easily be taken for a ride if you don't know just what you're after.

Szt. István körút 3. Tel: 131 4534
Felszabadulás tér 3. Tel: 118 3381
Andrássy út 27. Tel: 142 5525
Andrássy út 34. Tel: 132 5759
Kossuth Lajos út 1/3. Tel: 117 3718

There are also several small shops and stalls around Honvéd tér. Walk up the Szt. István körút from the M3 station of Nyugati pu in the direction of Margaret Island and then turn left. Here you'll find all manner of kitsch, but also the odd real rarity.

Stamps

SPECIAL SHOP FOR PHILATELISTS
Váci utca 63 (M3 Felszabadulás tér.)
The owner is a real expert and collector, and gives excellent advice. He also has some real rarities from the last century.

FILATELIA
Oktogon (M1 Oktogon)
Tel: 142 0948
Open Monday–Friday 8am–noon. Specialises in new series from Hungary and abroad, as well as stamps judged to be the 'year's best' by a special jury.

BÉLYEGMUZEUM (Stamp Museum)
Hársfa u. 47 (M2 Blaha L. tér)
Tel: 142 0960
Open Tuesday–Sunday 10am–6pm.

Art Galleries and Dealers

There can be hardly anything more exciting but also more risky than buying art. When purchasing the work of artists without a fixed international market value, you need to rely on your own aesthetics and keen eye. No amount of specialist advice can replace your own brave and spontaneous decisions.

GULACSY GALÉRIA
Tanács körút 6 (M2 Astoria)
Tel: 118 8933
The gallery was founded by an independent group of artists years ago, with the aim of exhibiting and selling their work. The mixture of styles and materials here gives visitors a good overall impression of Hungarian modern art.

QUALITAS GALÉRIA
Becsi u. 2 (all Metro lines: Deák tér)
Tel: 118 4438
The Pánno 2000 artist group has its paintings, graphics and sculptures on sale here. Hungarian art from the turn of the century onwards can be seen in the room at the back.

MONUMART
Szabad sajtó út 5 (M3 Felszabadulás tér.)
Tel: 117 1001
Open Tuesday–Saturday 10am–6pm. On the first floor, above the rather conventional 'Budapest Galéria', you can see some of the best modern art in Hungary.

MŰVÉSZ GALÉRIA
Rákóczi út 7 (M2 Astoria)
Tel: 118 1175
Open Monday–Friday 2–5pm. Contemporary cartoons, naive gypsy painting

PANDORA GALLERY
Iranyi u. 19 (M3 Felszabuladás tér)
Tel: 117 7709
Open Monday–Friday 10am–6pm, Saturday 10am–2pm. Art historian Péter Sinkovits has been running this gallery since 1991. It contains some of the best work of the past few decades.

TÖ GALÉRIA
Henger u. 2 (M2 Batthyány tér.)

Straw souvenirs

On the Buda side, at the foot of Rose Hill. A studio shared by several young artists.

ECSERI MARK FLEA MARKET
Nagykőrösy u. 156
Tel: 147 1364
Open Monday–Saturday 8am–3pm. In the XIX district, southeast of the city of Pest. Can be reached by M2 via Boráros tér – Keleti pu – West Station, by bus no. 54, or by car in direction of Kecskemét. Covers a huge area and is especially busy at weekends. Everything's been on offer here since 1964, from antiques to contraband. Haggling is quite normal, and a sensible thing to do. Snack bars make sure you'll never go hungry or thirsty. A speciality is the 'lángos', a kind of pita bread with garlic.

Arts and Crafts
Fine handmade goods, and textiles in particular, can be bought in Budapest very cheaply. Women refugees of Hungarian origin or immigrants from Transylvania in particular are real experts at traditional embroidery, and often offer their wares for sale at the roadside. There are also several hundred shops where not only textiles but also traditional wood-carvings and ceramics can be bought. Beware though: the range of goods on offer is huge, and you should distinguish carefully between machine-made kitsch and genuine, traditional handicraft before buying anything. Here's one safe tip, though:

MUZEUMI SOUVENIRBOLT
(Museums' Souvenir Shop)
Jószef nádor tér (M1 Vörös-marty tér.)
Here, just one block north of Vörösmarty tér, you can buy handmade copies of the finest exhibits from all the

Historical memorabilia

museums all over the country. Each individual piece is manufactured in limited quantities, usually in the same manner as the original; not cheap, therefore, but still definitely worth the money.

Market Halls
The Central Market Hall on the Pest side of the Freedom Bridge (also see *Day 3* in the *Day Itineraries* section) is worth a visit just for its picturesque stalls and its lively atmosphere. Recently renovated, it is a real gem of late 19th-century architecture.

CENTRAL MARKET HALL
Vámház körút 1–3 (M3 Kálvin tér)
Tel: 117 6865
Monday–Thursday 6am–4pm, Friday until 7pm, Saturday until 3pm.

Other weekly markets in Budapest are generally provided with their

wares by farmers and smallholders from outside the city, and the stallholders often sell their own produce.

The following markets are open weekdays 6am–6pm:

HOLD UTCA, in district V, in the northern part of Pest city.

BOSNYYAK TÉR, in district XIV, northeast of Pest.

FÉNY UTCA, near Moszkva tér, line M2, in the northwest of Buda.

The following markets are also open Sunday 6am–1pm:

BATTHYANY TÉR 2–6, Buda, right at the exit from the M2.

FEHÉRVARI UT, in district XI, in the southwestern part of Buda.

ÉLMUNKAS TÉR, in district XIII, north of Pest.

Shoes and Leather Goods

Leatherworking in Hungary dates back to the Magyars; no wonder, really, when you consider their nomadic origins. First-class leather goods can still be purchased in Hungary even today, though no longer at the wonderfully low prices common just a few years ago.

EKÉS GLOVES
Régiposta u. 14
Tel: 137 2465

PÉCSI KESZTYU GLOVES
Paulay Ede u. 39
Tel: 142 5926

DISZ TÉR 16
Buda, Tel: 175 0472

HABITUS
Semmelweis u. 2
(M2 Astoria)
Tel: 138 1058

VASS SHOES
Hariz köz
Just a few yards away from Váci utca. Handmade shoes and gloves; orders only take a few days.

Fashion

Alongside the fashion shops already familiar to visitors from the West, a few old-established stores have still managed to stay afloat:

CLARA SZALON
Váci utca 12
Tel: 118 4090
One of the most elegant salons for women in the whole city. Clothing also available made-to-measure.

MÉRETES NŐI DIVATSZALON
Károlyi Mihályi u. 7
Tel: 118 1428
Ladies' fashions made-to-measure; orders are usually processed within three days.

DAVID GMK
Váci utca 67 (M3 Felszabadulás tér)
Tel: 138 2371
Men's fashions, also made-to-measure.

BAMBOLA CHILDREN' BOUTIQUE
Galamb u. 5 (M1 Vörösmarty tér)
Tel: 137 4575

Traditional clothing

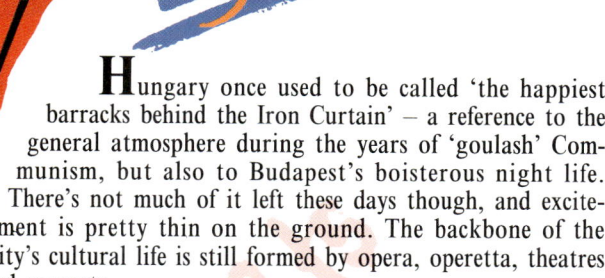

Nightlife

Hungary once used to be called 'the happiest barracks behind the Iron Curtain' – a reference to the general atmosphere during the years of 'goulash' Communism, but also to Budapest's boisterous night life. There's not much of it left these days though, and excitement is pretty thin on the ground. The backbone of the city's cultural life is still formed by opera, operetta, theatres and concerts.

Hungarian films, despite exciting productions from the latest generation of young film-makers, are not shown in any of the film clubs around the city, and have no chance against the tidal wave of Hollywood productions. A visit to one of the city's open-air cinemas in the summer, though, is still quite fun. Jazz, on the other hand, has a long local tradition and is still just as popular as ever.

A novelty are the discos that strive to live up to Western standards (or their own definition thereof), and apart from those a handful of traditional dance halls are still just about keeping their heads above water. A good general survey of what's on when can be obtained from the monthly magazine *Programmes in Hungary*, which can be found in most hotels. The English-language newspaper *Budapest Week* is even more up-to-date, and doesn't just reserve its praise for the big-budget shows. Locals, however, and those familiar with Hungarian, tend to rely first and foremost on *Pesti Műsor*, which has been appearing every Wednesday for four decades now, and contains all there is to do and see in the city within its 100 or so pages. Advance ticket sale outlets are at:

Moszkva tér, Tel: 135 9136. Open 11am–6pm.
Sütő utca 2 (Tourinform), Tel: 118 8718. Open 8am–8pm.
Andrássy út 18, Tel: 112 0000. Open 10am–5pm.

Festival poster

Classical Music / Light Music

OPERAHAZ (Opera House)
Andrássy út 22 (M1 Opera)
Tel: 131 2550 and 153 0170

NEMZETI SZINHAZ (National Theatre)
Hevesi S. tér (M2 Blaha L. tér)
Tel: 141 3849

OPERETT SZINHAZ (Operetta Theatre)
Nagymező utca 17 (M1 Kodaly körond)
Tel: 132 0535

MADACH SZINHAZ (Madach Music Theatre)
Erzsébet körút 29–33 (All Metro lines: Deák tér)
Tel: 122 2015

VIGADO
Vigadó tér 1 (M1 Vörösmarty tér)
Tel: 118 9903

BUDAI VIGADO
Corvin tér 8
Tel: 201 5928

ACADEMY OF MUSIC
Liszt Ferenc tér 8 (M1 November 7 tér)
Tel: 142 0179

BABSZINHAZ II (Puppet Theatre)
Andrássy út 69 (M1 Kodaly körönd)
Tel: 142 2702

CONGRESS CENTRE (Main Hall)
Jagèllo út 1–3 (M2 Terminus, Deli pu.)
Tel: 125 2869

FŐVAROSI MŰVELDŐSI HAZ
(Folklore Theatre)
Fehérvári út 47 (M3 Ferenc körút)
Tel: 181 1360

TRADITIONAL FOLKLORE DANCE HALLS
Tel: 142 4327
Information from the information service at Petőfi Hall of Culture.

Cinemas

Good original-language films from America, France and Germany can be seen at:

BROADWAY
Tanács körút 3, Tel: 122 0230
EUROPA
Rákóczi út 82, Tel: 122 5419
HORIZONT
Erzsébet körút 13, Tel: 122 2499
LUX
Arpád út 77, Tel: 169 2461
SZINDBAD
Szent István körút 16, Tel: 131 8673
TABAN
Krisztina körút 87–9, Tel: 156 8162

Music Clubs

MERLIN JAZZ CLUB
Gerlóczy u. 4
Tel: 117 9338
This venue in Pest City, open daily 6pm–2am, presents jazz, rock and the odd avant-garde theatre performance or cabaret act. Very friendly crowd, relaxed atmosphere and nice low

prices. Snack meals and drinks are also available.

PETŐFI CSARNOK (House of Culture and Music Hall)
Zichy utca 1–8 (M1 Hósök tere)
Tel: 142 4327
In the City Park. The 'in' place for young people, with a programme that changes weekly (rock, jazz, theatre performances). Lively and cheap.

FREGATT SÖRÖZÖ
Molnar u. 26
Tel: 118 9997
In Pest City, open 5pm–midnight. A pleasant cross between an English pub and a jazz club.

ROCK CAFÉ
Dohany u. 20 (M2 Blaha L. tér)
Open 6pm–4am. The best place to go for blues fans, and for lovers of traditional and hard rock. A popular meeting-place for the local youth, quite often noisy, but not aggressively so.

FEKETE LYUK (The Black Hole)
Ferenc körút (M3 Ferenc körút)
Only open Thursday to Sunday 8pm–3am. Pest's underground venue. Hard rock and live concerts given by such exotic groups as Vágtázó Halottkémek (The Galloping Undertakers). Lots of nice people, despite the rather martial decor.

CASABLANCA
Ferenc körút 19–21 (M3 Ferenc körút)
Tel: 114 2290
Open 9pm–3am. The 'in' disco of Budapest. Male visitors are given a thorough inspection by the bouncers, and there's free admission for women; yes, it's that kind of place!

GAY SERVICE/HOMERO'S DISCO AND DRINKS BAR
Akácfa utca (M2 Blaha L. tér)
Open daily 5pm–2am.

Poster by Rez-Diamant Sandor

Calendar of Special Events

Just as in other former Eastern bloc countries, the festival calendar in Hungary has undergone several rapid alterations ever since the fall of Communism. Anything remotely reminiscent of the Communist era has been done away with, especially the anniversary of the 'Great October Socialist Revolution' on 7 November. The new festivals reflect the country's own history. Important days in the Catholic calendar, too, such as Ascension Day and Corpus Christi, are also being increasingly re-adopted in Hungary, even though they have yet to be declared as public holidays.

Making a long weekend of things is one custom that hasn't changed though: if a public holiday happens to fall on a Tuesday or a Thursday, you can be sure that hardly anyone will be at work on the weekdays in between.

JANUARY/FEBRUARY

1 January: New Year's Day.
6 January: Epiphany; start of the Carnival season and the ball season.
13 February: Unofficial memorial day to mark the end of the siege of Budapest on 13 February 1945.
Mid-February: Hungarian Film Festival.

MARCH/APRIL

15 March: Anniversary of the 1848 uprising; memorial ceremony at the Petőfi Statue on the Corso.

End of March: Budapest Spring Festival with the motto: '10 days, 100 towns, 1,000 events' – includes classical and modern music, opera, ballet and theatre performances. Also a lot of exhibitions featuring international participation.
Easter Sunday/Monday: Traditionally a high holiday in Hungary.
4 April: Formerly a public holiday in memory of the end of World War II for Hungary, but today it still marks the beginning of the spring holidays and the start of the open-air season.

MAY/JUNE

1 May: Labour Day.
End of May: International Spring Fair for capital (unfinished) goods.
Last week in May: International Book Fair.

JULY/AUGUST

While theatres and concert halls close down for the summer, quite a few events are held out of doors. Open-air cinemas and rock and pop festivals provide varied entertainment.
20 August: St Stephen's Day, Hungary's first king and the founder of the Hungarian state. Parade in front of the Parliament Building, fireworks, and an amazing crush of people.

SEPTEMBER/OCTOBER

Third week in September: International Autumn Fair.
25 September: Béla Bartók's birthday, and the start of the Budapest Festival. Its many events and international guests liven up the city until the end of October.
23 October: Anniversary of the 1956 revolution. For three decades, Hungarians quietly commemorated their tragic failure to introduce reform and freedom of speech to the Communist system. On this day in 1989, Hungary was officially declared a republic.

NOVEMBER/DECEMBER

Vox-Pacis Choral Festival, with international choirs and organists in the city's concert halls and its – alas, often rather badly heated – churches.
6 December: St Nicholas' Day, popular with families and children.
Christmas is celebrated everywhere. Tourists who want to eat out on Christmas Eve should reserve well in advance. Many places close.
Last week of the year: several classical concerts take place.
New Year's Eve: Gala evening in the Vigadó, and fireworks above the city.

Festival celebrant

Practical Information

GETTING THERE

By Road

Travellers to Budapest will probably want to drive in through Vienna, from which a motorway (A4) leads almost to the crossing at Hegyeshalom. Listen to the radio if it is summer, as the crowds here can be quite substantial. As an alternative you can try the Klingenbach/Sopron crossing about 70km (40 miles) to the south of Vienna. At any rate there are more crossings further to the south. If driving through Carinthia in Austria, you may want to cut through Maribor, Slovenia (drivers here are several degrees worse than the Hungarians) and drive in through Letenye.

Motorists need a valid driving licence, a sticker showing which country they're from and also valid vehicle registration documents. The insurance green card isn't expressly required, but motoring organisations still recommend you bring one along, together with special vouchers that can be redeemed if your car needs to be towed home.

By Ship

The Hungarian MAHART company and the Austrian DDSG-Donaureisen company operate hydrofoils and ships between Vienna and Budapest (and elsewhere). The trip is picturesque but not necessarily cheap. In Budapest the ships tie up at Belgrád rakpart between Erzsébet and Szabadság bridges. Your local travel agent should be able to help you with information. You can also write to or call: DDSG-Donaureisen, Handelskai 265, A-1021 Vienna, Tel: 0222-217 500. Or try MAHART, Belgrád rakpart, Budapest V, Tel: 118 1704.

By train…

By Plane

Many airlines fly to Budapest's Ferihegy airport. MALÉV, Hungary's national airline, uses the Ferihegy II terminal, all others use Ferihegy I. I can recommend MALÉV. Recently Alitalia became a 35 percent shareholder in the airline and new routes are being planned, new planes bought (767s for long-distance flights). There are regular flights to and from all European capitals and major cities, several Balkan cities, a number of Middle Eastern cities (Damascus, Tel Aviv and Cairo, for example) and New York. Flight times are 1hr10 from Berlin, 1hr15 from Munich, 1hr50 from Amsterdam, 1hr55 from Paris, 2hr10 from London, 2hr25 from Helsinki, 2hr50 from Istanbul, 10hr25 from New York.

As well as its offices around the world (see *Useful Addresses*), MALÉV also has desks in the main Budapest hotels. Inter-

national airlines flying to Hungary have offices in Budapest as well, mainly near the centre (see also *Useful Addresses*).

Unfortunately the regular and inexpensive bus service linking the airport with Deák tér in Pest has recently been cancelled, although there may soon be a replacement. Current options are a shared minibus for approximately 600 Forint; it should drop you at your hotel or wherever you want. For the return trip you can order the minibus to pick you up at a given location. Call 157 8993. A taxi from the airport should cost around 1,600 Forint, inflation however is steep. Make sure the meter is running.

A final possibility is renting a car directly at the airport. Hertz and Avis, for example, have desks there. For good value, however, you will have to shop around. And do not forget to ask if prices include the value added tax (VAT) which is currently at a stratospheric 25 percent. (See *Car Rentals* below).

By Rail

The main railway line to Budapest from Western Europe runs via Vienna. A good dozen trains run daily between the two Danube capitals. Trains from the west, such as the Orient Express, usually arrive at the Keleti pályaudvár, the Eastern Station, in Budapest.

If you happen to be a national requiring a visa, you will have to get it before boarding the train. The other long-distance station is the West Station, Nyugati pályaudvár. The third main station in the capital, Déli pályaudvár, is on the Buda side in the eastern part of the city. From there the trains travel to Balaton and to southern Hungary.

For the trip from one station to another you should allow at least half an hour; the Metro is a lot faster than a cab. Timetable information in German or English: Tel: 131 5346.

TRAVEL ESSENTIALS

When to Visit

The best time to travel to Budapest is either the spring or the autumn; summer is extremely hot and winter can get very cold indeed. At all times, however, there's always a lot of cultural activity going on. Bear in mind that in winter the use of brown coal for heating will asphyxiate the untrained lung; fortunately, however, this is unlikely to effect the vast majority of visitors, who will be staying in centrally-heated hotels.

Passports and Customs

Europeans (except citizens of Portugal, Greece and Turkey), Americans, members of the CIS, Canadians, Argentinians no longer need to buy the $25 visa before entering Hungary. Most Asians, Middle Easterners and Latin Americans require visas, as do Australians, New Zealanders and Maltese.

No drugs or firearms (unless you are a hunter, and then you need a special permit

Traffic police

from the consulate in your home country) are allowed into the country. CB transmitters and car telephones have to be registered at the border. If you are 16 or older, you are allowed 250 cigarettes, or 50 cigars, or 250 grams of tobacco, two litres of wine or one litre of spirits. The exporting of food is limited, but no one seems to really check unless you are doing it by the lorry. However, your wallet may be checked for currency! You are not allowed to take out more than 500 Forint, though there is a degree of tolerance.

Residence permits information is obtainable from: Andrássy út 12. Office hours: Monday, Wednesday and Friday 9am–noon, Tuesday and Thursday 2–6pm, Tel: 118 667.

GETTING ACQUAINTED

The state of Hungary has been in existence for at least 1,000 years; the Parliamentary Republic of Hungary (Magyar Köztársaság) first came into being on 23 October 1989, the anniversary of the 1956 uprising.

Since 1989 the government has taken the form of a parliamentary democracy with two chambers. The highest authority in the land is the State President, who is strongly placed politically under the terms of the constitution, even with regard to the government in power, which is led by a prime minister.

Metropolitan Budapest has 2.2 million inhabitants, roughly a fifth of the country's population as a whole. A full 10 percent of the population is made up of ethnic minorities, the largest of which include Serbs, Croatians, Slovaks and Romanians. The city is divided up into 22 administrative districts, denoted by Roman numerals. The most important of them are I (Buda) and V (Pest City).

Time

CET (Central European Time), i.e. summertime is from the last weekend in April until the last weekend in September, and then the clocks are put forward an hour.

MONEY MATTERS

The Hungarian currency is the Forint (Ft), or the HUF for Eurocheque purposes. It divides up into 100 Fillér. The

A warm welcome

Forint comes in 5,000, 1,000, 500, 100, 50 bills; rare are 20 and 10 Forint bills. There are also 20, 10, 5, 2 and 1 Forint coins. The Fillér comes in lightweight aluminium units of 50, 20 and 10.

Hungary is currently cheaper than western countries, but inflation is high, ranging between 25 and 35 percent. The currency is frequently devalued as well. The Forint is not a convertible currency, therefore exchanging it back into a hard currency will be costly. Only change as much as you need. The symptom of inconvertibility is the fairly frequent occurrence of money changers who offer better exchange rates on the street. These transactions are illegal. Furthermore, the money changers are often shady fellows, who work in gangs. It is better to avoid them, for if you are bamboozled by one of them, you have no legal recourse.

Eurocheques can be cashed in banks and most post offices to a maximum of 15,000Ft. The acceptance of credit cards is also spreading rapidly – but not to all petrol stations.

Tipping

Gratuities are included in the price, but it's usual to add an extra 10 percent of the final sum as a tip anyhow.

GETTING AROUND

The Metro

In operation daily 4.30am–11.10pm. You can buy single tickets for one trip from the termini, at tobacconists and also from Metro kiosks in the pedestrian subways. You have to punch your ticket yourself in the train. Day tickets aren't worth buying; you only really start sav-

ing with monthly ones. Budapest has three Metro lines.

The M1 line serves the north-eastern part of Pest and runs from Vörösmarty tér below the Andrássy út as far as the City Park. The terminus is Mexicói út.

The M2 runs from west to east, from the South Station (Déli pu) on the Buda side to Batthyány tér (where the suburban railway line HÉV departs for Óbuda and Szentendre), and then on to the East Station (Keleti pu) before reaching Örs vezér tér. From there the HÉV travels on to Gödölló and the Hungaroring.

The M3 travels north-south, down the Pest side, from Árpád híd station through

the centre of Pest to Kóbánya-Kispest and the terminal for the two airports Ferihegy I (international flights) and Ferihegy II (domestic flights with MALÉV). All three Metro lines intersect beneath Deák tér in the centre of Pest.

Buses and Trams

In the city both buses and trams cost the same as the Metro and run at the same times; some trams and blue buses run at night. Bus No 78 takes roughly the same route as the M2, and bus No 182 that of the M3.

The lines with red numbers are express bus lines, only stopping at important traffic intersections.

For other forms of transport there's also the nostalgic funicular railway (Sikló) up to the Castle from the bank of the Danube (daily 7.30am–10pm), the rack railway from Sziagyi Erzsébet fasor in the northwestern part of Buda on Buda Hill (daily 4.30am–midnight, approximate journey time 25 minutes), and the Libegó chairlift to the Janós-hegy observation point in the eastern part of the city (daily 9am–5pm, journey time 15 minutes).

Taxis

Taxis with their signs illuminated are for hire. The tinnier makes of car such as Dacia or Lada are generally cheaper than Mercedes or BMWs. Calling a cab by telephone is possible, and most drivers speak a little English and German. They're very happy to do longer trips for you, but make sure you negotiate a fixed price in advance (rule of thumb: a good car plus driver for a full day costs around $75).
Fötaxi, Tel: 118 8888
Volantaxi, Tel: 166 6666
Budataxi, Tel: 120 0200
Gabrieltaxi, Tel: 155 5000

Public Transport

Yellow buses do the long-distance routes. Most of them leave from Erzsébet tér, near Deák tér. Timetables and price lists are available daily 5.30am–9pm by calling 117 2511 or 117 2369.

Hungarian Rail (MAV) has an extensive rail network but is comparatively expensive. **National Information** (daily 6am–9pm), Tel: 122 7860 or 142 9150.
International Information, Tel: 122 4052.
MAV **customer service office**: VI, Andrássy út 35 (Monday–Friday 9am–5pm), Tel: 122 8049 and 122 8056.
Sleeping car reservations can be made at **Utasellato**: Tel: 114 0803.

Driving

The road system is quite good, and around Budapest are several sections of motorway. Information on traffic conditions can be obtained from Utinform: Budapest VI, Andrássy út 11. Tel: 122 7052.
The Highway Code is largely similar to that of Western Europe. Note the following, though:
• **Alcohol** at the wheel is strictly forbidden, as is sounding your horn in any built-up areas.
• **Seat belts** are compulsory; motor-cyclists must wear helmets.
• **Children** may only travel in the back seat.
• **maximum speed** permitted: 50 kph (30 mph) in built-up areas, 80 kph (50 mph) on country roads, 100 kph (60 mph) on trunk roads and 120 kph (75 mph) on motorways.

Petrol

Normal is 86 Octane, Super 92, and Extra 96. Lead-free petrol *(ólomentes* – 95 octane) is increasingly to be found on all trunk roads and at least a dozen filling stations in Budapest. Diesel *(Dízel)* is of average quality.

Breakdown Services

Emergency Phone Numbers: 169 1831, 169 3714, 183 4580, 183 4572.
The 'Yellow Angels' of the Hungarian Automobile Club will help you or organise any repairs.
Hungarian Autoclub: Francia út 38, Tel: 169 1831.
Camping and Caravan Club: Múzeum utca 11, Tel: 114 1880.

Traffic

Traffic in Budapest is hectic and undisciplined. For information, including help with any difficulties you may encounter, ring the Hungarian Autoclub:
Information: Tel: 112 6218, 132 6500.
Customer and Breakdown Service: Tel: 169 1831, 169 3714, 183 4580, 183 4572.
Customer Service: Visegrádi u. 17. Tel: 132 2650.
Other services: Rómer Flóris u. 4a. Tel: 115 2040.
'Yellow Angel' Breakdown Service: Tel: 169 1831, 160 3714, 183 4572.

Car Rental

You have to be at least 21 to hire a car, and you'll need your national driving licence plus your passport. Credit cards are accepted. The rates for a small car are around $50 a day. Advance reservation

in your home country often makes things a lot cheaper. Almost all firms offer special weekend rates.
Avis/Ibusz: Martinelli tér 8, Tel: 118 6222; at the airport Tel: 145 5574.
Cooptourist/Budget: Ferenc körút 43, Tel: 113 1466.
Hertz: Kertész u. 24, Tel: 111 6116; at Airport I – Tel: 157 9123.
Europcar/Volantourist: Vaskapu u. 16, Tel: 133 4783; at Airport I – Tel: 134 2540; at Airport II – Tel: 157 8519.

HOURS & HOLIDAYS

Business Hours

Times tend to vary here, and all that can be said is that, generally, shop trading hours are Monday–Friday 8am–7pm and Saturday 8am–1pm, with some shopping centres open on Sunday as well. Museums are open Tuesday–Sunday 10am–6pm, and mostly closed Monday.

Public Holidays

1 January: New Year's Day
15 March: National Holiday (comemmorating the 1848 Revolution)
1 May: Labour Day
20 August: St Stephen's Day
23 October: Memorial day for the 1956 uprising, and anniversary of the birth of the Republic in 1989.
25/26 December: Christmas.

ACCOMMODATION

Hotelkeeping in Budapest has a long tradition, and the prices, too, are on a par with those of Western Europe. Landlords also advertise their rooms privately ($15–40 per night) via agencies at airports, railway stations and approach roads, and sometimes even personally.

Budapest has a tradition of hotel-keeping

Recommended Hotels

GRAND HOTEL RAMADA ☆☆☆☆
Margitsziget
Tel: 111 1000, Fax: 153 3029
Superbly situated on Margaret Island, double rooms from about $140.

HILTON HOTEL ☆☆☆☆
Hess András tér
Tel: 175 1000, Fax: 156 0285
A praiseworthily-designed modern structure right on Castle Hill.

GELLÉRT HOTEL ☆☆☆
Szent Gellért tér 1
Tel: 185 2200, Fax: 166 6631
Classic spa hotel with direct access to the famous thermal baths. Double rooms from around $140.

ASTORIA ☆☆☆
Kossuth Lajos u. 19
Tel: 117 3411, Fax: 118 6798
A nostalgic old building with a superb restaurant right at the heart of Pest City, and therefore rather noisy. Double rooms from $130.

TUSCULANUM HOTEL ☆☆
Záhony u. 10
Tel: 188 7673, Fax: 168 7773
In Óbuda. Modern, quiet, cheap. Double rooms from $50.

FLANDRIA HOTEL ☆
Szegedi út 27
Tel: 129 6689
North of the City Park, easily reached via the M1. Double rooms from $25.

ANANDA – Private Hostel
Bonyhádi út 18/b
Ten minutes from Eastern Station (Kerepesi utca) on trolley bus No 80. Nine stops later, alight at Mályva utca. Reception open 6am–3am. Cheap and clean.

Apartments

ANDRAS SZILAGYI
Mosolygó Antal utca 64
Fax and Tel: 272 3388
Mr Szilágyi has 4-, 3-, and 2-bed apartments near the centre, and rooms in his own house. Prices up to $22 per person.

Camping

For information contact the **Magyar Camping és Caravanning Club**, Kálvin tér 9, Tel: 118 5259.

HARSHEGY
Hárshegy u. 517
Tel: 176 1921
Region II, in the north-western part of the city.

ROMAI FÜRDŐ
Szentendrei u. 189
Tel: 168 6260
In the northern part of Óbuda near the Roman remains.

FLORA HOTEL KEMPING
Kazinczy u. 105
Tel: 185 6071

FORTUNA
Dósza Gy. u. 164
Tel: 166 4364

HEALTH & EMERGENCIES

Doctors

First aid and doctors' visits have to be paid for, mostly in foreign currency. Medical aid is available around the clock from the following clinics:

IMS Outpatient Clinic: Váci utca 202, Tel: 149 9349.

Trauma Institute: Lörcy Sandor u. 3–5, Tel: 133 5593.

Children's Clinic: Üllői út 86, Tel: 133 0718.

Dentex dental practice: Városligeti (Gorki fasor) 32, Tel: 142 4257.

Gellért doorman

Accidents

Helicopter Rescue Service **Aerocaritas**: Tel: 62-53 130 and 62-53 950.

Accidents have to be reported to the police immediately, and forms need to be filled out even for minor collisions. Report any accident – even if it wasn't your fault – immediately to **Hungária Insurance Budapest**, Gvadányi út 69, Tel: 252 6333.

Pharmacies (Gyógyszertár)

Almost all strong medicine is only available on prescription. Payment must be made in cash. The normal opening times are Monday–Friday 8am–8pm, Saturday 8am–2pm. On Sunday and public holidays and at night the following pharmacies remain open:

II, Frankel Leó út 22. Tel: 115 8290
III, Szentendrei út 2a. Tel: 188 6528
IV, Pozsonyi u. 19. Tel: 189 4079
VI, Teréz körút 95. Tel: 111 4439
VII, Rákóczi út 86. Tel: 122 9613
VIII, Szigony út 2. Tel: 113 5870
IX, Üllői út 121. Tel: 133 8947

Emergency Numbers

These key numbers can be dialled from any telephone:
Emergency Rescue Service: 04
First Aid: 04
Fire Brigade: 05
Police: 07

COMMUNICATIONS & NEWS

Post

Post offices are open Monday–Friday 8am–6pm (except in smaller towns and villages) and 8am–2pm (at the latest) on Saturday.

The post offices at the West and East train stations in Budapest are open all night and Sunday. At the Central Post Office – Petőfi S. utca, 7am–7pm – you can also send and receive faxes and telexes (Telex: 225 375 plebl Bp., Fax: 117 0170).

Stamps range in value from 1–100 Forint. A postcard to Western Europe currently costs 30 Forint, a letter 40 Forint, and there's a surcharge of 30 Forint for express air mail.

Important Phone Numbers:
Information: 118 6977
Information in foreign languages: 117 2200, 117 0170, 117 0000
Round-the-Clock Information: 117 0100
Wake-up service: 117 2522

Telephone

Public telephone boxes in Hungary come in varying colours: the metallic ones are for local calls only (5 Forint) and calls within Hungary (dialling code 06), and the red ones are more suitable for international calls. You need 5, 10 or 20 Forint coins though – and lots of them. It's a better idea to buy a phone card at the post office. Remember, too, that telephoning is cheaper between 6pm and 7am, and also at weekends.

To dial internationally, press 00 and wait for the tone. Useful country codes: Australia (61); Canada and United States (1); Germany (49); Italy (39); Japan (81); the Netherlands (31); Spain (34); UK (44). If you wish to use a US phone card, dial the company's access numbers are: AT&T 00-360111; MCI 00-800 01411; Sprint 00-800 01877.

Courier Services

Boy Szolgálat: V, Bajcsy Zs. utca 20. Tel: 132 3523 (for 24-hour freight services); 132 3522 (for courier services); 132 3521 (for advance ticket sales – opera, theatre, circus).
Tnt – Malév Express: next to the Hyatt Atrium Hotel in the Apaczai Cs. J. utca. Tel: 266 5122, 266 2164, and also at the airport.
Dhl: Rákóczi út, in the Business Centre opposite the Hotel Astoria. Tel: 185 2082, 185 2085.

MEDIA

The best – and most accurate – source of tourist information is *Budapest Week*, a weekly magazine in English compiled by Hungarians and foreigners. Also, at hotel receptions and tourist agencies, there are monthlies such as *Programme in Hungary*, containing a great deal of advertising. International newspapers and magazines can be bought from street vendors or at the larger hotels.

The Petőfi station on FM does the news in German and English at noon every day. As far as TV is concerned, international programmes can be received via satellite, as can the news in English and German.

LANGUAGE

Hungarian belongs to the Finno-Ugric family of languages. Its only relations in Europe are Finnish and Estonian. It is, however, sheer myth that the Hungarians and Finns understand each other. Barring a handful of ancient words recalling a common past (such as *vaj* for butter), only linguists can explain the link.

Learning Hungarian can be fun. In Hungarian words, the stress is always on the first syllable. The accent on, say, Andrássy, is thus not a stress mark, it just lengthens the vowel slightly. Beware of pronunciations:

a = a as in car
á = open a as in after

c = ts
e = e as in especially
é = a as in bare (distinction of e and the long é is very important: *segg* means bottom, and *ség*, see the salutation below, is a common suffix: eg. *hidegség* means cold, *hidegseg* means cold bottom).
gy = a run together dyuh
i = short ee
í = long ee
ly = long i with a sound, a kind of yuh
ny = a kind of nyuh
ty = a slightly aspirated tyuh (tyuk = tee-ook)
o = short o as in horror
ó = long o as in Poland
ö = e as in perfect
ő = same as ö but longer
s = sh
sz = s
u = oo
ú = oooo
ü = same as in German, or u in French
ű = same as ü but longer
zs = who does not know Zsa-zsa Gabor?

The language is agglutinative, which means two things. First you stick prepositions, personal articles, and a variety of case suffixes at the end of the word. The result is, for example, "Healthyourto!" (*Egészségünkre*!).

Like the Germans, Hungarians also stick words together with particularly lengthy results: *fagylaltkülönlegességek* means ice cream specialties. Verbs, on the other hand, come apart, but not with Germanic regularity. Among the strangest floating particles is the famous *meg* indicating a completed action. Unfortunately all this complication means that there is little room for a pidgin-Hungarian, since the juxtaposition of undeclined verbs and nouns gives no meaning.

The Akadémiai Kiadó publishes a nice little Hungarian-English dictionary that you can find in most larger bookstores in Hungary. Cost is minimal, and it will help you plough through menus, headlines and some museum titles. However hard it may seem, Hungarians will always be pleased that you have tried to understand their language.

Common Words and Phrases

Try a little talking

Yes, no	*Igen, nem*
Pardon (apology, eg)	*Bocsánat*
Excuse me (what time is it? eg)	*Elnézést*
Good morning!	*Jó reggelt kívánok*
Good day!	*Jó napot kívánok*
Good evening!	*Jó estét kívánok*
Good night!	*Jó éjszakát kívánok*
Goodbye!	*Viszontlátásra* (colloquially *visz'lát*)
Bon appétit!	*Jó étvágyat kívánok*

Please	*kérem szépen*
Thank you	*köszönöm szépen*
How much is it?	*Mennyibe kerül?*
Is there… ?	*Van… ?*
I'd like to pay	*fizetni (kérem)*
Where is… ?	*Hol… ?*
left	*balra*
right	*jobbra*
straight	*egyenesen*
Naturally	*persze*

Hotel	*hotel, szálloda*
Double/single room	*kétágyás/egyágyás szoba*
Bathroom	*Fürdszoba*
Toilet	*WC, toalett, mosdó*
Ladies/gents	*női/férfi*
Shop	*bolt, üzlet*
Price	*ár*
closed/open	*zárva/nyítva*

Help	*segítség!*
Doctor	*orvos*
Ambulance	*Mentőauto*

Police	*rendőrség*
Leave me alone	*Hagyj békén* (fairly polite)

Counting = *Egy, kettő, három, négy, öt, hat, hét, nyolc, kilenc, tíz. Tizenegy, tizenkettő,… Húsz, harminc, negyven, ötven, hatvan, hétven, nyolcvan, kilencven, szász* (100). *Ezer* (1,000).

Days: Monday to Sunday: *hétfő, kedd, szerda, csütörtök, péntek, szombat, vásárnap.*

Finally, a frequently heard word is *tessék*. It is universally applied and can mean please (inviting you to help yourself); it is the way to answer a telephone, a waiter will approach you with the words *tessék parancsolni* (please, order); it can also mean 'there you go' as in proving a point.

SPORT & LEISURE

Bowling: Hotel Novotel, XII, Alkotás utca 63–67. Tel: 166 5635.
Squash: City Squash Club, II, Marcibányi tér 13. Tel: 135 2518.
Riding: Metro Tennis Camping, XVI, Csömöri út 158. Tel: 163 8505. Petneházy Country Club, II, Feketefej utca 2–4. Tel: 176 6992.
Tennis: SAS Club Hotel, XIII, Törölbálinti utca 51–53. Tel: 166 9899. Flamenco Tennis, XI, Bartók Béla út 63. Tel: 166 5699.

Films and Photography

Films and cassettes of all the major makes are cheap in Hungary. Development within two days is no longer a problem either, though as usual repairs are still something of a sore spot.

The zoo – small but charming

The main photo shops are **Ofotért** or **Főfoto**; there are also **Photo-Porst** at Váci utca 7, open Monday–Friday 9am–6pm, Saturday 9am–4pm; **Agfa Minilab**, Ferenc körút 3, or the Hungarian-American firm of **Fotex** at Váci utca 9, open Monday–Saturday 9am–9pm and Sunday 10am–9pm.

Zoo

Budapest's small but charming zoo (XIV, Allatkerti utca 6–12, Tel: 142 6303) is near the City Park on the yellow M1 line (get off at Hösök tere). Open daily 10am–4pm, and 9am–6pm in summer. There's a palm house, a terrarium, a crocodile hall, a bird house, an elephant house and a giraffe house here, all waiting to be visited. Plant fans will adore the orchid house and the collection of cacti. There are also pony rides for children in summer.

USEFUL ADDRESSES

Tourist Offices

Ibusz is Hungary's long-standing travel agent, and it has now been privatised. It has offices in many parts of the world:
Chicago: Ibusz, 233 North Michigan Ave, Suite 1308, Chicago, Illinois 60601, Tel: (312) 819-3150.
London: Danube Travel Ltd, 6, Conduit Street, London W1R 9TG, Tel: (71) 493-0263.
New York: Ibusz, One Parker Plaza, Suite 1104, Fort Lee, New Jersey 07024, Tel: (201) 592-8585.
Tourist offices are omnipresent in Hungary, beginning with border crossings, the airport, train stations. They provide numerous services including making hotel reservations, changing money, etc. Don't expect to always find up-to-date brochures. If you are staying in a more expensive hotel, you will probably have a tourist office located somewhere in the lobby. A vital number in Hungary is the international Tourist Information Service **Tourinform** in Budapest, Sütő utca 2, on Deák tér. Tel: 117 9800. Use it in Budapest, or the following:
Budapest Tourist
Roosevelt tér 5, Tel: 117 3555

Cooptourist
Kossuth L. tér 13-15, Tel: 112 1017
Hungarotours
Akácfa utca 20, Tel: 141 3889
Ibusz Hotel Service
Petőfi tér 3, Tel: 118 5707

Foreign Embassies in Budapest

Austria
VI, Benczúr utca 16. Tel: 121 3213
Germany
XIV, Stefánia út 101–103. Tel: 251 8999
Consulate: Nógrádi utca 8, Tel: 155 9366
Switzerland
XIV, Stefánia út 107. Tel: 122 9491
UK
V, Harmincad utca 6. Tel: 118 2888
US
V, Szabadság tér 12. Tel: 112 6450

Airlines

Malév offices

Malév maintains a number of offices world wide.
Canada: Toronto, Tel: (416) 944-0093
Israel: Tel: 972/3/524 6171
UK: London, Tel: (71) 439-0577
US: New York, Tel: (212) 757-6480, toll free: (800) 223 6884; Chicago, Tel: (312) 819 5353; Los Angeles, Tel: (310) 286 7980.
In Hungary, most travel agents are in touch with the airline.

Airlines in Budapest

Malév
Roosevelt tér 2, Tel: 118 4333, 118 9033; at the airport Tel: 157 8406 (arrivals), 157 8768 (departures).

Lufthansa
Váci utca 19, Tel: 118 4511.
At the airport Tel: 157 0290.

Austrian Airlines
Régiposta u. 5, Tel: 117 1550. At the airport Tel: 167 4374.

Air Canada
I, Sziklai u. 1, Tel: 175 4618.

Someone to help

Swissair
Krisztóf tér 7–8, Tel: 117 2806.
At the airport Tel: 157 4374.

Air France
Krisztóf tér 6, Tel: 118 0411.
At the airport Tel: 157 1663.

British Airways
V. Apáczai Csere János u. 5, Tel: 118 3299 and 118 3041.

Flight information in Budapest
General Information Tel: 157 9123.
Daily flights Tel: 157 7155 and 157 7743.

Lost & Found
Whatever you lose and wherever you lose it, try ringing one of these numbers:

Public Transport
BKV, Akácfa utca 18. Tel: 122 6613.

Railway stations and trains
Keleti pu, Tel: 122 5615; Nyugati pu, Tel: 149 0115; Delí pu, Tel: 175 9485.

On the street
Central Police Commissariat, Deák Ferenc utca 16–18. Tel: 118 0080.

Traveller's cheques and credit cards
Hungarian National Bank, Tel: 153 260.

FURTHER READING

Apa Publications, *Insight Guide Hungary* (2nd edition 1991), a comprehensive guide to the history, culture and sights.

László Cseke, *The Danube Bend* (1977; originally published in Hungarian, 1976), explores the beautiful Danube landscape to the north of the city.

C A Macartney, *Hungary: A Short History* (1962) contains information on the capital.

Ferenc Molnár, *The Paul Street Boys* (1907). A classic work of Hungarian literature.

Gyula Németh (ed), *Hungary: A Complete Guide*, translation from the Hungarian, 3rd revised edition (1988), discusses the history and environs of the city.

Martyn C Rady, *Medieval Buda: A Study of Municipal Government and Jurisdiction in the Kingdom of Hungary* (1985), the most authoritative work on the subject.

T I Berend and G Ránki, *Hungary: A Century of Economic Development* (1974), contains information on the capital.

Emeric W Trencsényi (comp.), *British Travellers in Old Budapest* (1937), a collection of descriptions of the city beginning with Edward Brown in the 17th century.

Photography	**Hansjörg Künzel** *and*
Pages 17, 20	**Hans Skupy**
18, 26, 29, 30, 31, 32, 35т,	**Marton Radkai**
41, 42, 52, 53, 54, 57т, 57в,	
58, 61в, 63, 64, 65, 67, 68,	
69в, 87, 90	
22, 27, 28, 35в, 36,	**Alfred Horn**
37, 45, 50, 59, 61т, 62, 71,	
77, 79, 87	
Production Editor	**Erich Meyer**
Cover Design	**Klaus Geisler**
Handwriting	**V. Barl**
Cartography	**Berndtson & Berndtson**

INSIGHT GUIDES

160 Alaska
155 Alsace
150 Amazon Wildlife
116 America, South
173 American Southwest
158A Amsterdam
260 Argentina
287 Asia, East
207 Asia, South
262 Asia, South East
194 Asian Wildlife,
     Southeast
167A Athens
272 Australia
263 Austria
188 Bahamas
206 Bali Baru
107 Baltic States
246A Bangkok
292 Barbados
219B Barcelona
187 Bay of Naples
234A Beijing
109 Belgium
135A Berlin
217 Bermuda
100A Boston
127 Brazil
178 Brittany
109A Brussels
144A Budapest
260A Buenos Aires
213 Burgundy
268A Cairo
247B Calcutta
275 California
180 California, Northern
161 California, Southern
237 Canada
162 Caribbean
     The Lesser Antilles
122 Catalonia
     (Costa Brava)
141 Channel Islands
184C Chicago
151 Chile
234 China
135E Cologne
119 Continental Europe
189 Corsica
281 Costa Rica
291 Cote d'Azur
165 Crete
184 Crossing America
226 Cyprus
114 Czechoslovakia
247A Delhi, Jaipur, Agra
238 Denmark
135B Dresden
142B Dublin
135F Düsseldorf

204 East African Wildlife
149 Eastern Europe,
118 Ecuador
148A Edinburgh
268 Egypt
123 Finland
209B Florence
243 Florida
154 France
135C Frankfurt
208 Gambia & Senegal
135 Germany
148B Glasgow
279 Gran Canaria
169 Great Barrier Reef
124 Great Britain
167 Greece
166 Greek Islands
135G Hamburg
240 Hawaii
193 Himalaya, Western
196 Hong Kong
144 Hungary
256 Iceland
247 India
212 India, South
128 Indian Wildlife
143 Indonesia
142 Ireland
252 Israel
236A Istanbul
209 Italy
213 Jamaica
278 Japan
266 Java
252A Jerusalem-Tel Aviv
203A Kathmandu
270 Kenya
300 Korea
202A Lisbon
258 Loire Valley
124A London
275A Los Angeles
201 Madeira
219A Madrid
145 Malaysia
157 Mallorca & Ibiza
117 Malta
272B Melbourne
285 Mexico
285A Mexico City
243A Miami
237B Montreal
235 Morocco
101A Moscow
135D Munich
211 Myanmar (Burma)
259 Namibia
269 Native America
203 Nepal
158 Netherlands

100 New England
184E New Orleans
184F New York City
133 New York State
293 New Zealand
265 Nile, The
120 Norway
124B Oxford
147 Pacific Northwest
205 Pakistan
154A Paris
249 Peru
184B Philadelphia
222 Philippines
115 Poland
202 Portugal
114A Prague
153 Provence
156 Puerto Rico
250 Rajasthan
177 Rhine
127A Rio de Janeiro
172 Rockies
209A Rome
101 Russia
275B San Francisco
130 Sardinia
148 Scotland
184D Seattle
261 Sicily
159 Singapore
257 South Africa
264 South Tyrol
219 Spain
220 Spain, Southern
105 Sri Lanka
101B St Petersburg
170 Sweden
232 Switzerland
272 Sydney
175 Taiwan
112 Tenerife
186 Texas
246 Thailand
278A Tokyo
139 Trinidad & Tobago
113 Tunisia
236 Turkey
171 Turkish Coast
210 Tuscany
174 Umbria
237A Vancouver
198 Venezuela
209C Venice
263A Vienna
255 Vietnam
267 Wales
184C Washington DC
183 Waterways
     of Europe
215 Yemen

You'll find the colorset number on the spine of each Insight Guide.